NATIONAL GEOGRAPHIC
Reach
for Reading
COMMON CORE PROGRAM

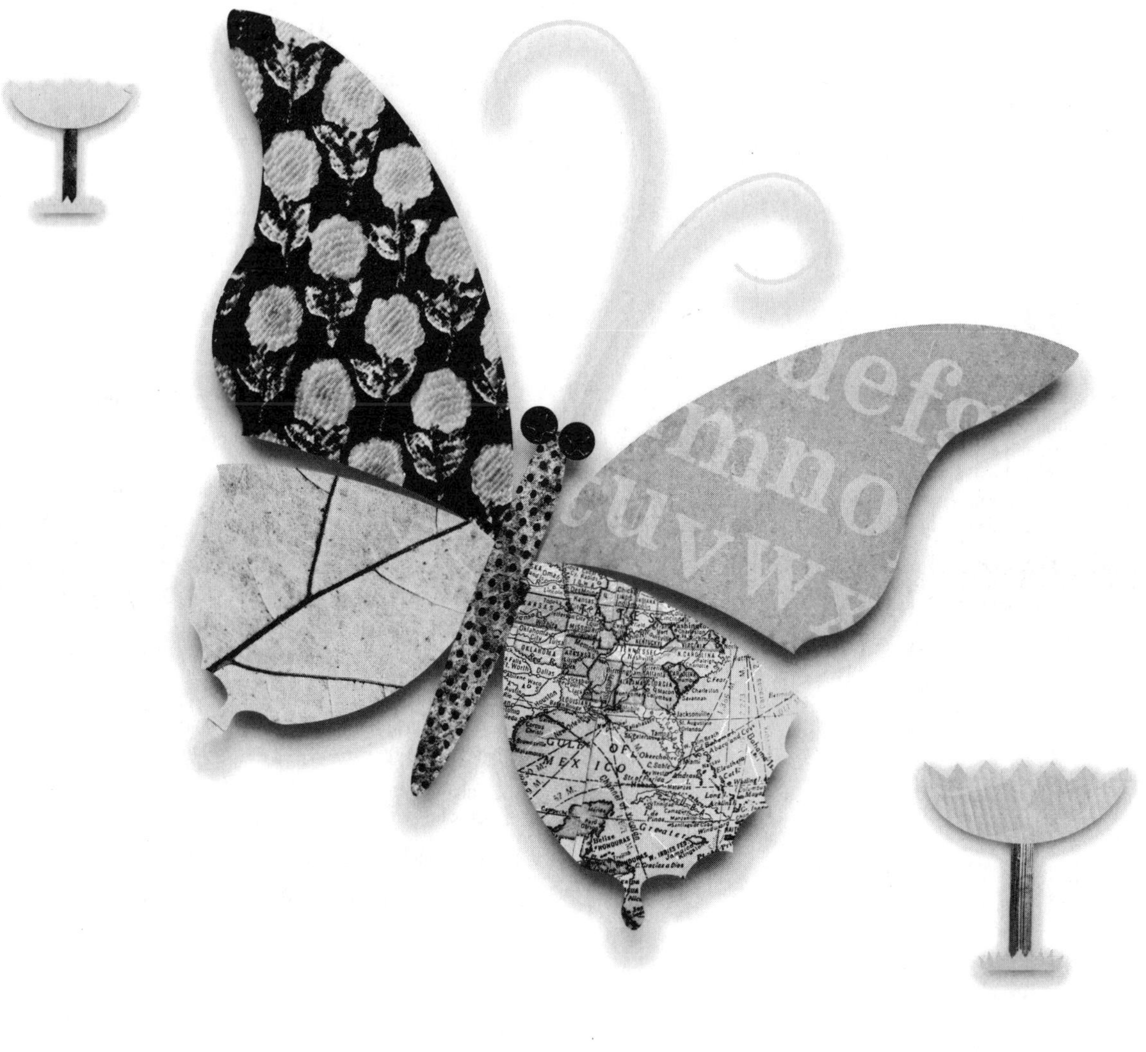

NATIONAL GEOGRAPHIC

Hampton-Brown

Acknowledgments

Grateful acknowledgment is given to the authors, artists, photographers, museums, publishers, and agents for permission to reprint copyrighted material. Every effort has been made to secure the appropriate permission. If any omissions have been made or if corrections are required, please contact the Publisher.

Cover Design and Art Direction: Visual Asylum

Cover Illustration: Joel Sotelo

Visit National Geographic Learning online at www.NGSP.com

Visit our corporate website at www.cengage.com

Printed in the USA.

Printer: RR Donnelley, Harrisonburg, VA

ISBN: 978-11338-99648

12 13 14 15 16 17 18 19 20 21

10 9 8 7 6 5 4 3 2 1

Contents

Contents, continued

Contents, continued

Name ____________________ Date ____________

Unit Concept Map

Living Traditions

Make a concept map with the answers to the Big Question.

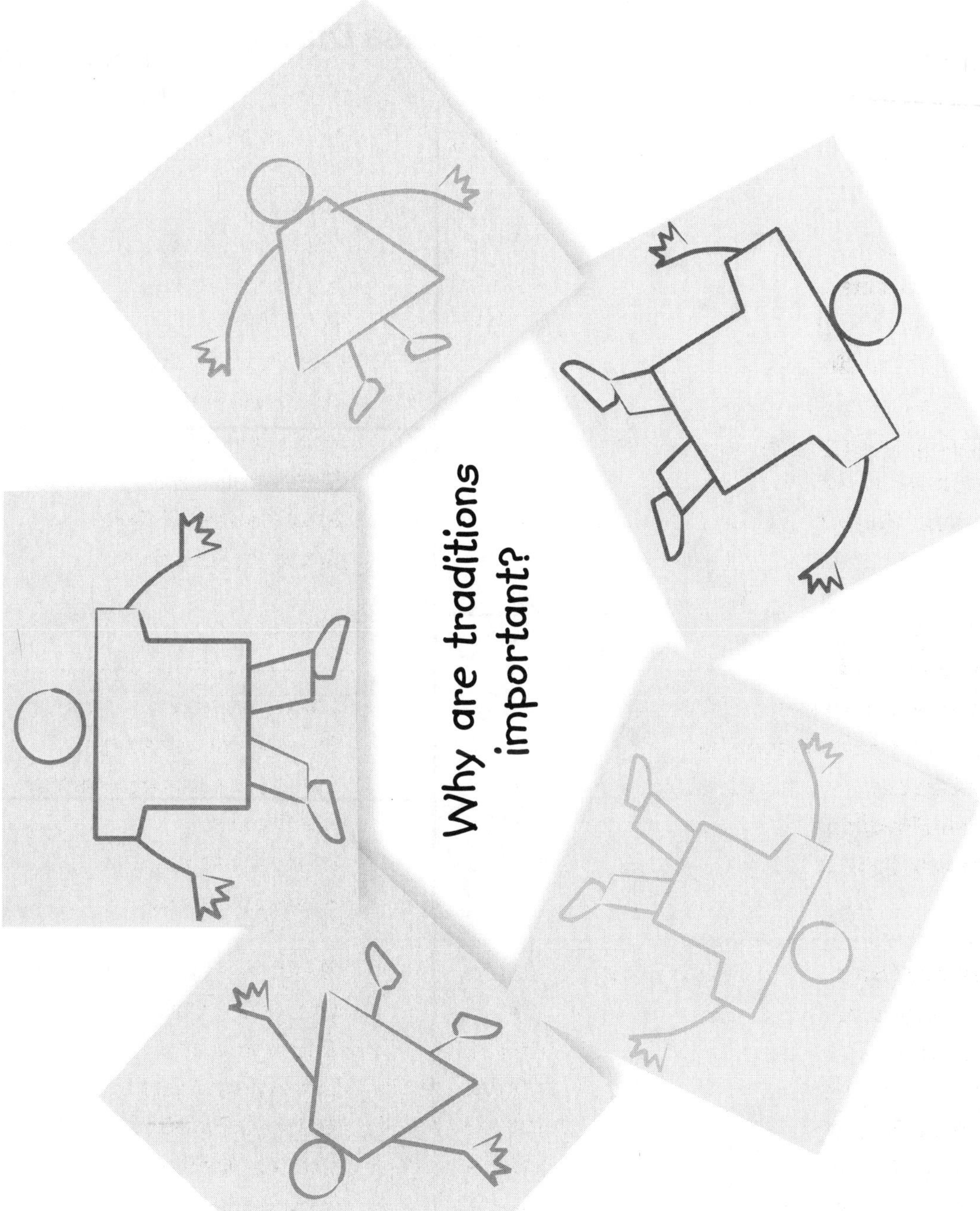
Why are traditions important?

Main Idea Diagram

Street Fair

Make a main idea diagram ~~about the photo of~~ a ~~street~~ fair/festival ~~on page~~ that you have been to.

Main Idea

Main Idea Diagram

Details

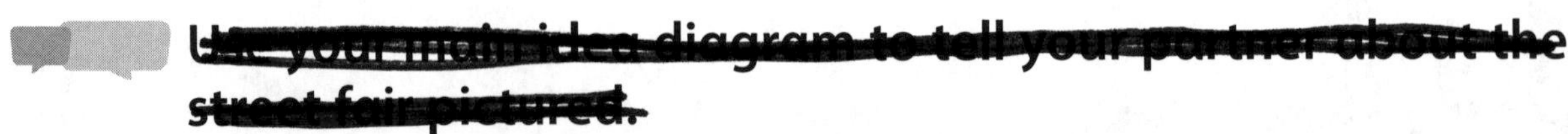

~~Use your main idea diagram to tell your partner about the street fair pictured.~~

PM1.2

What Am I?

Think of a person who takes part in a tradition and write clues about that person in the circle. Each clue should follow the sentence type listed. Have your partner use the clues to guess the answer.

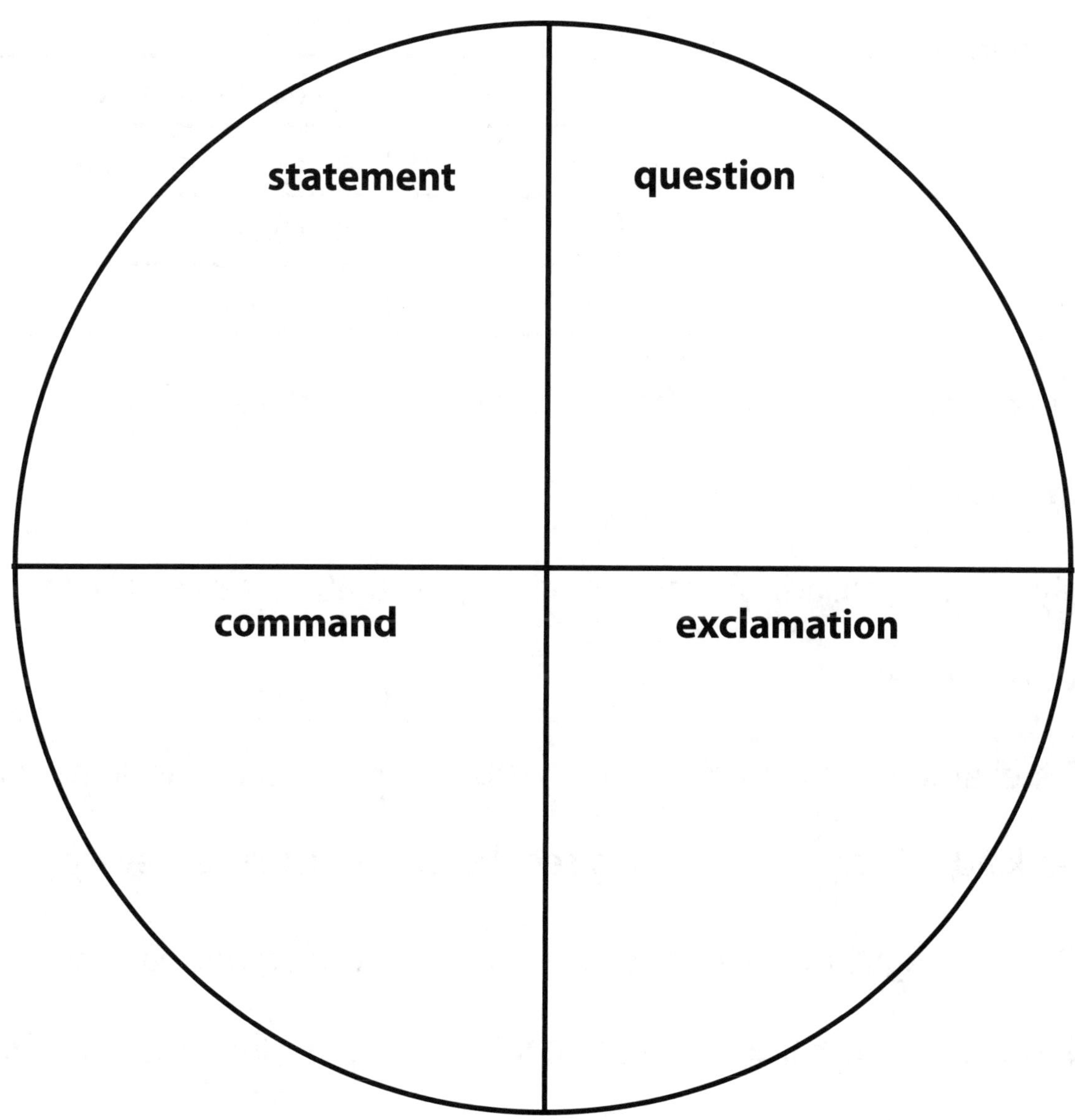

Edit and Proofread

Choose the Editing and Proofreading Marks you need to correct the passage. Look for correct usage of the following:

- incomplete sentences
- subject-verb agreement
- capitalization
- end punctuation

Editing and Proofreading Marks

∧	Add.
ℰ	Take out.
⟨?⟩	Add question mark.
⟨!⟩	Add exclamation mark.
∧,	Add comma.
⊙	Add period.

How does your family celebrate traditional holidays⟨?⟩ Tell you about mine.

My family is Italian. we have special foods that we serve at different times of the year.

For example, on New Year's Eve we don't eats meat. Our dinner has seven kinds of fish. I can't wait to see the beautiful platters every year?

On Thanksgiving, my dad roast a turkey, but my grandpa also makes pasta with a special sauce that his father taught him to make.

On the Fourth of July, we have a cookout. why is the Fourth of July different in my family? Grandpa makes his special pasta and sauce, too!

Know the Test Format

Read the question about "Josh Ponte: A Musical Journey." Choose the best answer.

Sample

> **1** Which of the following is a musical instrument that is not seen or played very often any more in Gabon?
>
> Ⓐ mongongo
>
> ● pluri arc
>
> Ⓒ violin
>
> Ⓓ Gabonese harp

2 Why did Josh Ponte go to Gabon the first time?

Ⓐ He wanted to spend time in nature.

Ⓑ He was studying musical instruments.

Ⓒ He was forming a band.

Ⓓ He wanted to help the gorillas.

3 Describe one way the people of Gabon keep their traditions alive.

____

4 Mr. Ponte likes the way the Gabonese people live. Write a paragraph explaining several things he likes about how they live.

____

____

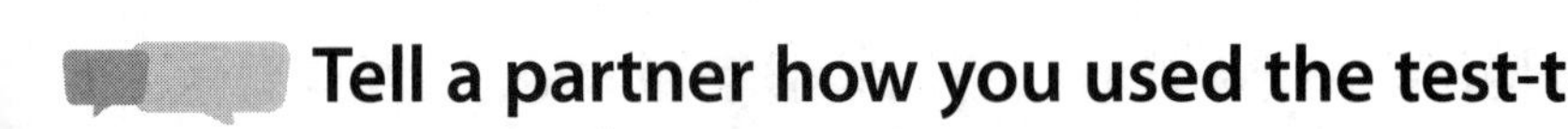 **Tell a partner how you used the test-taking strategy to answer the question.**

Unit 1 | Living Traditions

"Josh Ponte: A Musical Journey"

Main Idea Diagram

He was interested in nature.

Pages 12-13:
Ponte went to Gabon.

Use your main idea diagram to tell your partner what the interview was mainly about.

PM1.6

Fluency Practice

"Josh Ponte: A Musical Journey"

**Phrasing is how you use your voice to group words together.
Use this passage to practice reading with proper phrasing.**

Ramona: Why do you think people in Gabon care so deeply about the   13

natural world?   15

Mr. Ponte: I think it is because their traditions and lives are   27

connected to the natural world. The village is like a family.   38

The natural world provides them with everything   45

they need to live. They get their food from nature. They build their   58

musical instruments and homes from natural materials.   65

From "Josh Ponte: A Musical Journey," page 24.

Expression

1 ☐ Rarely pauses while reading the text.   3 ☐ Frequently pauses at appropriate points in the text.

2 ☐ Occasionally pauses while reading the text.   4 ☐ Consistently pauses at all appropriate points in the text.

Accuracy and Rate Formula
Use the formula to measure a reader's accuracy and rate while reading aloud.

_________ − _________ = _________
words attempted   number of errors   words correct per minute
in one minute   (wcpm)

It's All in a Day

Grammar Rules: Sentences

A **complete sentence** tells a complete thought. It has a <u>subject</u> and a <u>predicate</u>. The subject is who or what the sentence is about. The predicate tells something about the subject.	<u>My dog</u> <u>likes to run in the park</u>.
There are four kinds of sentences: **statement:** tell something **exclamation:** shows strong feeling **command:** tells you to do something **question:** asks something	Turtles are my favorite animal. That giraffe is very tall! Pick up the leash. Do you go to the zoo?

Read each sentence. Circle the subject. Underline the predicate. Identify each type of sentence on the line.

1. My class visits the museum. _______________________
2. Mr. Thomas shows us the dinosaur bones. _______________
3. The fossils look over five hundred years old! _______________
4. Did you see any other animals? _______________
5. Jackson digs for ancient jewels. _______________________
6. We learn many new things! _______________

 **Tell a partner three things you did today using a variety of complete sentences.**

Grammar: Game

Fragments to Sentences

1. **With a partner, cut apart the cards on the page.**

2. **Take turns drawing cards and turning the fragments into complete sentences.**

3. **Each time your partner agrees that the sentence you have created is complete, you get a point.**

4. **Play until all the fragments have been changed to complete sentences.**

5. **The player with more points wins.**

Many different colors.	Forms the clay into the shape of a bowl.	After the sculptor carves designs.
From different cultures.	If the clay is too hard.	When the clay dries.
Presses the clay with feet and hands.	The talented native artist.	A great love of sculpting.

Grammar: Game

It Depends

1. **Toss a marker onto a square. Read the sentence aloud.**
2. **Find the dependent clause and say the word that begins it.**
3. **Play until all the squares have been used.**

Many statues are made of marble, which can be pink, white, or other colors.

We saw the pottery of Hara Kiyoshi, who is a famous Japanese artist.

Reynald Joseph is a Haitian painter whose art is very colorful.

This silver jewelry is part of a collection that is famous throughout the world.

Before glass artists create glass marbles, they must heat the glass over a very hot flame.

These marbles, which come from Germany, are my favorites.

Some artists make sculptures by melting together pieces of junk metal that come from old cars.

Our Aunt Jan, whom we love to visit, always takes us to art museums.

Compare Author's Purpose

Comparison Chart		
	"Josh Ponte: A Musical Journey"	"Shaped by Tradition"
genre	interview	
author's purpose	to inform about Gabon's musical traditions	
stated? yes/no	yes	
If yes, where? If not, how can you figure it out?		

 **Take turns with a partner. Ask each other questions about the authors' purposes.**

Grammar Rules Complete Sentences

1. A **sentence** is a complete thought.
   It has a complete subject and a complete predicate.
2. The **complete subject** tells whom or what the sentence is about.
3. The **complete predicate** tells what the subject is, has, or does.

Read each group of words. Write *complete* if the words are a complete sentence. If it is not complete, tell what is missing.

1. Sixteen friendly gorillas   *missing predicate*

2. Sing while they work   _________________

3. Young people mix styles of music   _________________

4. Josh Ponte films people in Gabon   _________________

5. Some Gabonese people   _________________

Make each incomplete sentence above a complete sentence. Add a complete subject or a complete predicate.

____

____

____

Make two sentences with the same subjects. Have your partner combine them into one sentence with a compound subject.

Reviving an Ancient Tradition

by Ellen Wayne

Imagine winning a prize at a World's Fair! In 1933, the pottery of two Native American artists did just that at the Chicago World's Fair. Who were these amazing artists? María Montoya and Julian Martínez lived in the San Ildefonso Pueblo in New Mexico. Around 1908, they began perfecting an ancient pueblo pottery style that would make them world-famous.

In about 1887, María was born into a family of potters. When she was very young, she began making clay pots. María built her early pots from red or tan clay and painted them with traditional designs such as plants, feathers, or mountains.

As a young woman, María worked hard to become a skillful potter even though few people made pots in the pueblo. During María's teenage years, inexpensive metal pots were replacing clay cookware, so fewer people wanted to buy pottery. María's family made little money selling their pots, but they kept making pottery because they thought it was an important part of their culture.

After getting married in 1904, María and Julian began working together to create beautiful pots and jars.

▲ María and Julian revived this ancient design.

Reviving an Ancient Tradition (continued)

In 1908, archaeologist Edgar Hewett found some ancient black-on-black pottery shards at an old abandoned pueblo. He asked María and Julian to recreate this traditional style of their ancestors to display in his museum. María and Julian tried many different firing techniques. After several years of trial and error, Julian finally figured it out!

When people saw the Martínezes' black-on-black pottery in Hewett's museum, they wanted to buy similar pieces. It became so popular, other potters in the pueblo wanted to learn the method. They began teaching others in the pueblo during the 1920s.

The Martínezes continued making pots for the rest of their lives. María and Julian's

descendants have continued to make black-on-black pottery—even five generations later! With so many dedicated potters, it is unlikely that the ancient tradition of creating black-on-black pottery will ever be forgotten again.

▲ María became a skilled potter.

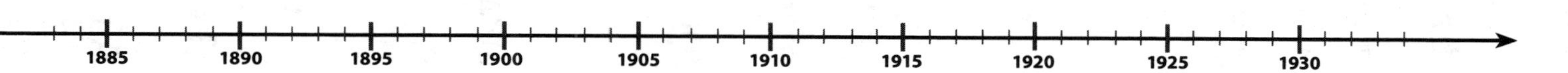

Grammar: Grammar and Writing

Edit and Proofread

Choose the Editing and Proofreading Marks you need to correct the passage. Look for and correct the following:

- sentence fragments
- capitalization
- end punctuation

Editing and Proofreading Marks

∧	Add.
⸜	Take out.
/	Make lowercase.
∧‚	Add comma.
⊙	Add period.

There is great museum in our state capital. That represents the many cultures in our state. It is called the Heritage Museum Our class took a trip there last week.

So many amazing kinds of art. We saw lovely baskets woven from swamp cane and palmetto. There was a display of little statues. That were carved by immigrants from South America.

On the second floor were paintings of ancient Greek buildings. The paintings were made by artists who came here from Greece. an African sculpture exhibit outside. This was my favorite exhibit.

You should visit this museum. Because it shows how many different types of people add beauty to our great state.

Painting Lesson

Grammar Rules: Fragments

A **fragment** is not a complete sentence. It does not tell a complete thought.	**Fragment:** Before the artist finished **Complete sentence:** Before the artist finished, he added his signature to the painting.
A dependent clause has a subject and a predicate, but it is not a sentence. It can begin with words like _before, after, because, when,_ and _if._ It can also begin with _who, whose, whom, which,_ or _that._	<u>If you don't like the movie,</u> we don't have to stay.

Underline the dependent clause in each item.

1. I learned how to paint because my sister taught me.
2. If she hadn't taught me, I would have taken a class.
3. I want to show my paintings when I am ready.
4. I will show them at the library, which supports local artists.
5. After all this, I may become famous!

Write three dependent clauses on a sheet of paper. Exchange it with a partner. Have your partner make the fragments into complete sentences.

Unit 1 | Living Traditions

Plot of a Story

Work with a partner. Tell each other a story. Make a story map to tell the plot of your partner's story.

Story Map

Beginning

↓

Middle

↓

End

 **Use the story map to retell your partner's story.**

Unit 1 | Living Traditions

Grammar: Game

Who, Whose, Whom?

1. Cut the cards apart and place the gray cards face up in a row. Place the white sentence cards face down in a pile.

2. Choose a card from the sentence pile.

3. Read the sentence aloud. Then choose the gray card with the correct relative pronoun to complete the sentence. Read aloud your sentence.

4. Have your partner continue by choosing a card from the sentence pile and completing that sentence.

5. Play until all the sentence cards have been used.

who	whose	whom
We learned about Pueblo pottery from Mrs. Martinez, _______ we visited at the museum.	Mom took me to hear David Broza, _______ sings Israeli music.	These luminaries are for my sisters, _______ give wonderful parties.
I like to visit Uncle Roger, _______ legends from Jamaica are my favorite stories.	We love to listen to Chris, _______ hands pound the bongos.	This hand-knit sweater is from Grandpa, _______ we see every winter.

Edit and Proofread

Choose the Editing and Proofreading Marks you need to correct the passage. Look for and correct the following:

- relative pronouns
- capitalization

Editing and Proofreading Marks

∧	Add.
℘	Take out.
⌒∧	Move to here.
∧,	Add comma.
⊙	Add period.

Traditional celebrations *are* part of people's cultural heritage.

are important to many people. Every culture has special celebrations

which are passed down through generations.

Some cultures special wedding traditions. For example, some

Russian families give crowns to the bride and groom, whose they

treat like royalty. At some Japanese weddings, the bride, who face is

painted white, wears a white kimono.

Some Polish celebrations include polka music, is very lively. Many

polka bands have a leader whom is an accordion player.

Know the Test Format

Read the passage. Then read the question and fill in the correct answer.

The Coffee Test

(1) In the folk tale "Martina the Beautiful Cockroach." (2) Abuela gives Martina advice about choosing a husband. (3) She tells Martina to spill coffee on her suitors' shoes. (4) A suitor who reacts badly will not make a good husband.

1 Which group of words is an incomplete sentence?

Ⓐ Group 1

Ⓑ Group 2

Ⓒ Group 3

Ⓓ Group 4

2 Martina did not want Don Gallo to be her husband because he was __________ .

Ⓐ quiet and calm

Ⓑ kind and giving

Ⓒ selfish and mean

Ⓓ loud and confusing

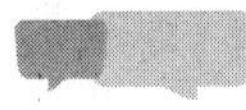 **How did you use the test-taking strategy to answer the question?**

Story Map

"Martina the Beautiful Cockroach"

Complete the story map to tell what happens in "Martina the Beautiful Cockroach."

Story Map

Beginning

Martina decides she is ready to get married. Abuela tells Martina about the Coffee Test.

↓

Middle

↓

End

Use your story map to retell the story to a partner.

"Martina the Beautiful Cockroach"

Expression in reading is how you use your voice to express feeling. Use this passage to practice reading with proper expression.

"*¡Gronc! ¡Gronc!*" squealed Don Cerdo as he dabbed at the   10

coffee on his shoes. "What a tragedy for my poor loafers!"   21

He really is quite a ham, thought Martina.   29

"Calm yourself, señor. I'll clean them for you!"   37

"I'll say you will!" he snorted. "When you are my wife, there'll   49

be no end to cleaning up after me!"   57

Martina rolled her eyes in disbelief.   63

"A most charming offer, señor," she said dryly, "but I must   74

decline. You are much too boorish for me."   82

From "Martina the Beautiful Cockroach," page 50

Expression

1 ☐ Does not read with feeling.

2 ☐ Reads with some feeling, but does not match content.

3 ☐ Reads with appropriate feeling for most content.

4 ☐ Reads with appropriate feeling for all content.

Accuracy and Rate Formula

Use the formula to measure a reader's accuracy and rate while reading aloud.

_____________ − _____________ = _____________
words attempted   number of errors   words correct per minute
 in one minute   (wcpm)

The Vet

Grammar Rules: Pronouns

Use **relative pronouns** to connect a dependent clause to a noun in the main clause.	This is a picture of my dog, who weighs one hundred pounds.
Use *who* to describe something, *whom* if it is receiving action, and *whose* to show possession.	This is my dog, who is seven years old. I have to take my dog to the vet, whom I like very much.
Use *that* to identify something in the main clause. Use *which* to add information about something in the main clause.	The vet took X-rays that will show the injury. My dog's paw, which is injured, will heal.

Circle the correct relative pronoun to complete each sentence.

1. This is my veterinarian Nina, (who/whom) I have known for years.
2. I recommended her to my neighbors, (who/whom) have a sick horse.
3. Nina gave them a bandage (which/that) was made from soft fabric.
4. We worried about the horse, (whom/whose) hoof hurt.
5. The hoof, (which/that) is bandaged, will mend.

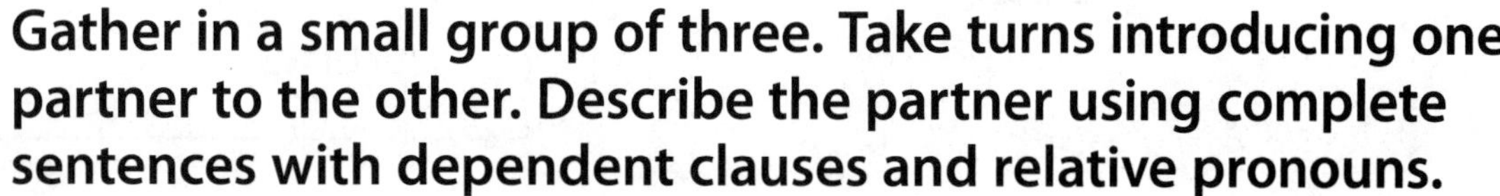

Gather in a small group of three. Take turns introducing one partner to the other. Describe the partner using complete sentences with dependent clauses and relative pronouns.

Grammar: Game

Spin-a-Clause

Make a Spinner

1. **Push a brad through the center of the circle. Open the brad in the back. Hook a paper clip over the top of the brad to make a spinner.**

2. **Follow the directions to play the game.**

Directions

- Spin the spinner and say the word it points to.
- Then choose a sentence from the box below. Use the word to add a dependent clause to one of the sentences.
- Take turns and continue playing until everyone has had at least three spins.

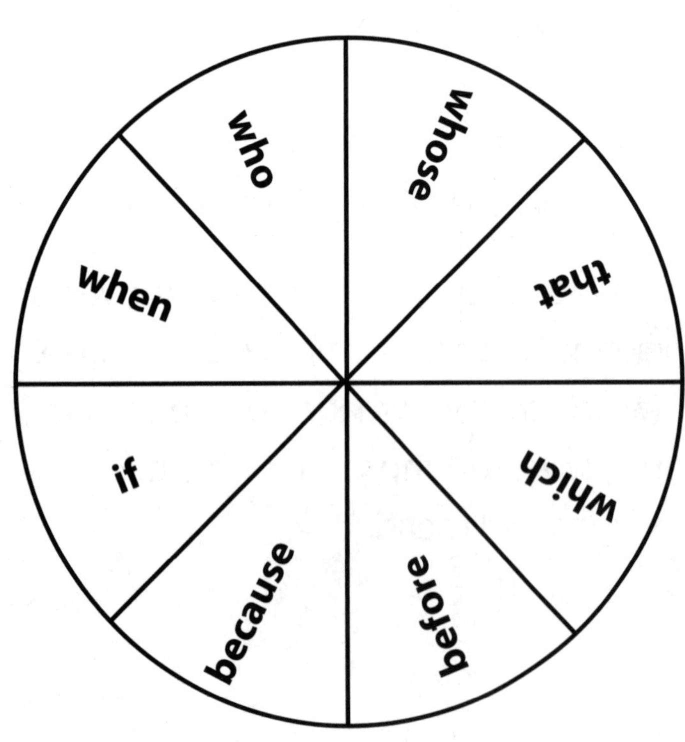

1. I always watch the Caribbean Heritage parade.
2. Arnetta learned how to weave from Aunt Deniece.
3. The *arepas* are from my cousin Hugo.
4. Laura taught me to make lasagna.
5. We listened to folk songs sung by our teacher.
6. The Navajo dance was performed for our parents.

Celebrate!

With a partner, make up a new holiday that your families could celebrate. Prepare sentences that tell about the holiday:

- Cut out the sentence fragments and gray labels. Place the three gray labels face up in a row.
- Together, sort the sentence fragments under the three labels.
- Take turns selecting fragments and adding the missing parts. Make sure all subjects and verbs agree.
- When all the sentences are complete, arrange them to create a description of your holiday to share with the class.

FRAGMENT Missing part: Subject	FRAGMENT Missing part: Predicate	FRAGMENT Dependent Clause

Our holiday's name _______________________________________.

This holiday celebrates _________________________________.

_______________ is the most delicious food served at our holiday.

Before we wake up ____________________________________.

When our holiday comes, _______________________________.

_______________ because this celebration is important to us.

Compare Content

Complete the Venn diagram to compare and contrast "Martina the Beautiful Cockroach" and "Coming of Age."

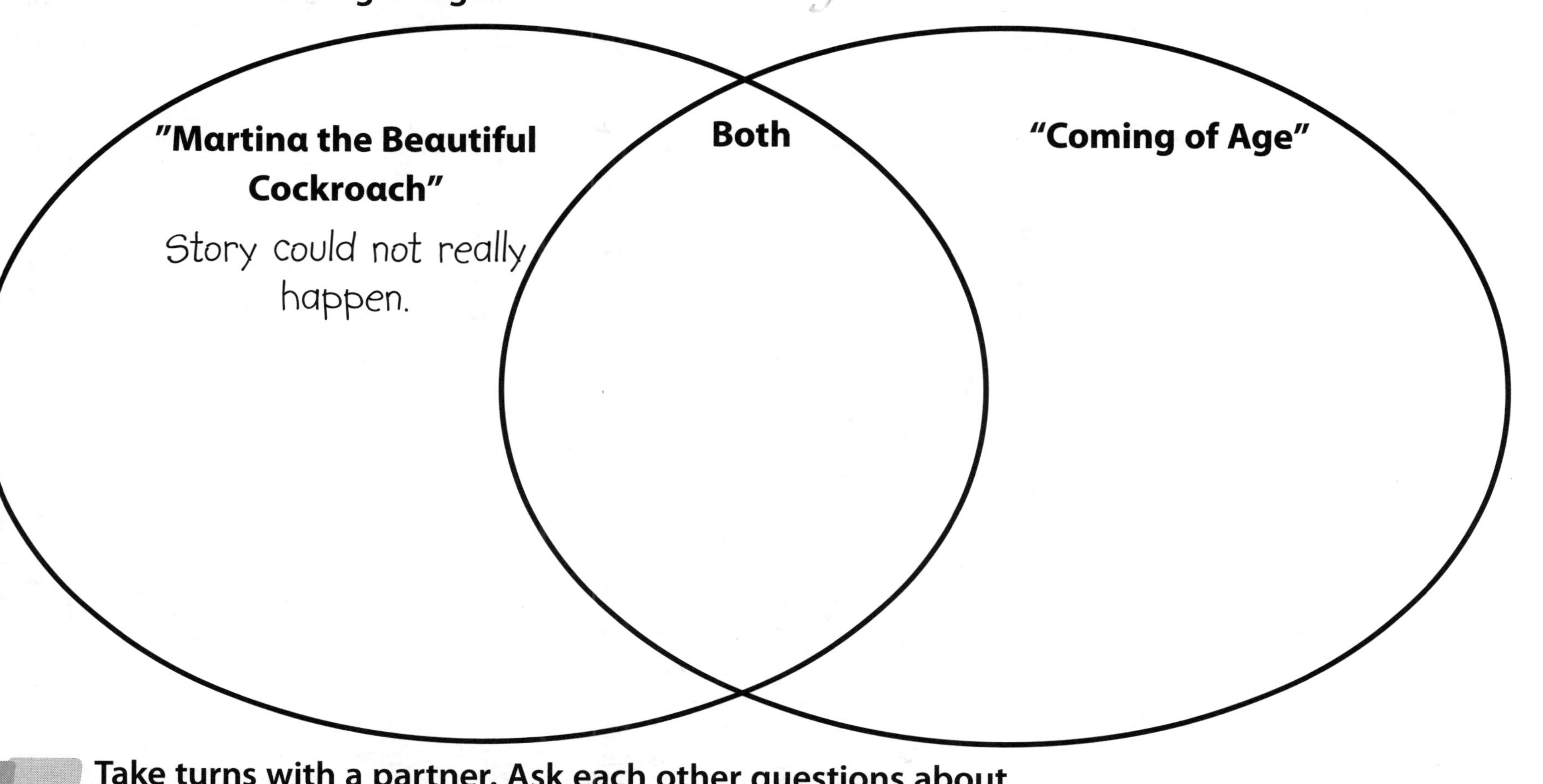

Take turns with a partner. Ask each other questions about the content of the two selections.

For use with TE p. T63a

PM1.26

Grammar Rules Subject-Verb Agreement

When a **subject** has two or more nouns joined by **and** or **or**, it is called a **compound subject**.

The **son** and the **daughter sit** on chairs.

Either the **son** or the **daughter sits** on a special chair.

The **son** or the **daughters sit** on a bench.

How do you know what verb to use with a compound subject?

If you see **and**, use a plural verb like *sit*.

If you see **or**, look at the last simple subject.

- Is it singular? Then use a singular verb like *sits*.
- Is it plural? Then use a plural verb like *sit*.

Write the correct form of the verb on the line.

1. My family and I ___celebrate___ important phases in life.
(celebrate)

2. My best friend and relatives _______________ me into adulthood.
(welcome)

3. My aunt and my uncle _______________ my first voni to me.
(present)

4. My aunts or my sister _______________ me gifts.
(hand)

5. Some women or guests _______________ saris to the ceremony.
(wear)

Talk with a partner about special occasions you have shared with other people. Use compound subjects in some of your sentences.

Chiyo and Naoki by Asami Oshii

"Good morning, Naoki!" Chiyo beamed. "Can you believe it? It's finally *Seijin no Hi*!"

Naoki smiled at his big sister. Today was the second Monday in January, which meant it was *Seijin no Hi*, or the coming-of-age day in Japan. Many of the young people turning 20 this year were busy preparing for the big event.

Naoki smiled at Chiyo with admiration. Their mother placed a bowl of *sekihan* on the table and began to chat excitedly with Naoki's grandmother about the day's festivities. They would leave soon for the beauty salon, where Chiyo would be dressed in a long-sleeved *furisode kimono*.

Naoki gazed out the window of their tiny apartment. He imagined 20-year-olds from around the cramped city gathering in the public auditorium for the *Seijin no Hi* ceremony.

"Are you on pins and needles, Big Sister?" asked Naoki.

"No, I'm on top of the world!" said Chiyo. "After today, I will finally be an adult. Everyone has to grow up!"

Everyone has to grow up. Naoki suddenly realized that their relationship was about to change. "Big Sister, after you become an adult today, will you still help me with my homework every night?"

Chiyo bit her lip. "I'll be busier now, Naoki, but I'll try."

Chiyo and Naoki (continued)

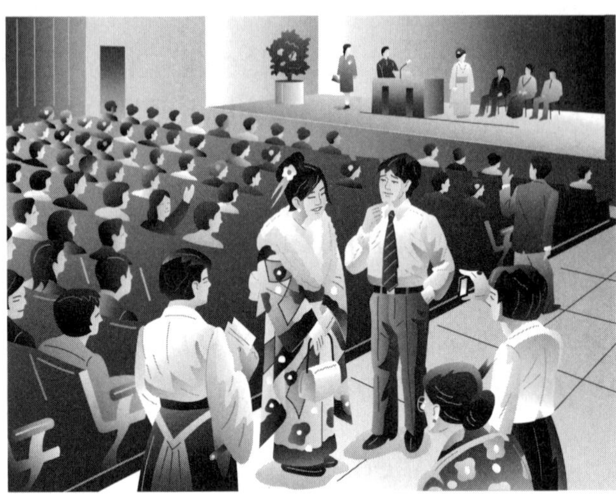

Chiyo's excitement built as she and her family arrived at the auditorium. The huge hall was filled to overflowing. Everyone in the community wanted to be part of the important event. The town leaders gave lengthy speeches, welcoming the young people into adulthood.

The young people, looking festive in their fine clothes, were seated at the front of the auditorium. Some young men wore traditional Japanese *hakamas*, but most wore formal modern suits. Many of the girls were dressed in colorful *kimonos* according to the custom. Even Naoki felt handsome in his new suit.

After the ceremony, Naoki sat at a low table to do his homework. In the past Chiyo had been there to help him, but tonight she was out celebrating. Naoki tried to focus, but he felt a touch of sadness. All of a sudden, he heard the door slide open.

"Big Sister! I'm so happy you're here. I was afraid you wouldn't want to spend time with me anymore now that you're an adult."

Chiyo smiled. "Don't be silly. Part of being an adult is realizing what is really important. And my family is what is important to me! My heart is still in the right place."

What do the details about setting tell you about what is important to the community? Review the text and art and explain your answer.

____

____

Edit and Proofread

Choose the Editing and Proofreading Marks you need to correct the passage. Look for the following:

- subject-verb agreement
- sentence fragments
- dependent clauses

Editing and Proofreading Marks

∧	Add.
⸜	Take out.
⟟∧	Move to here.
∧̖	Add comma.
⊙	Add period.

My parents and I loves to attend the heritage parades in our city. There seems to be a different one every week!

The Cuban parade is lively and colorful. The best music. Sometimes Dad dance as the bands pass by.

Another favorite is the parade for India. The beautiful saris and bracelets sparkles in the sun. Mom enjoy the musicians, whose play interesting instruments.

The parade I like most is the one which celebrates Greek heritage. The flags and the floats is all in blue and white. Most of the marchers wears traditional costumes. I usually buys a treat from the food vendor, whom has a Greek flag painted on his face.

The Big Parade

Grammar Rules: Compounds

A **compound subject** has two subjects joined by *and* or *or*.	Jaden <u>and</u> Jesse march in the parade every year.
The subject and verb of a sentence must agree. • If you see *and*, use a plural verb. • If you see *or*, look at the last simple subject. • If it is singular, then use a singular verb. • If it is plural, then use a plural verb.	Rebecca <u>and</u> Reece <u>ride</u> on the float. Renee <u>or</u> the <u>clown</u> <u>blows</u> the horn. The dog <u>or</u> <u>cats</u> <u>jump</u> through the hoop.

Write the correct form of the verb on the line.

1. Jenna and Maria ____________ the float after school.
   (build)

2. My grandfather or grandmother ____________ fruit and water.
   (bring)

3. Jose and Mark ____________ on the dance.
   (work)

4. My aunts or uncles ____________ the animals.
   (train)

5. The principal or teacher ____________ the float to the parade.
   (drive)

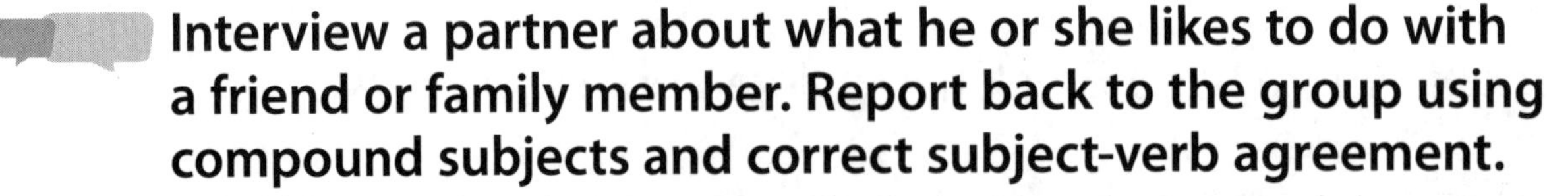

Interview a partner about what he or she likes to do with a friend or family member. Report back to the group using compound subjects and correct subject-verb agreement.

Animal Intelligence

Make a concept map with the answers to the Big Question:
Just how smart are animals? Write your ideas on the bodies of the ducks.

Smart things animals can do . . .

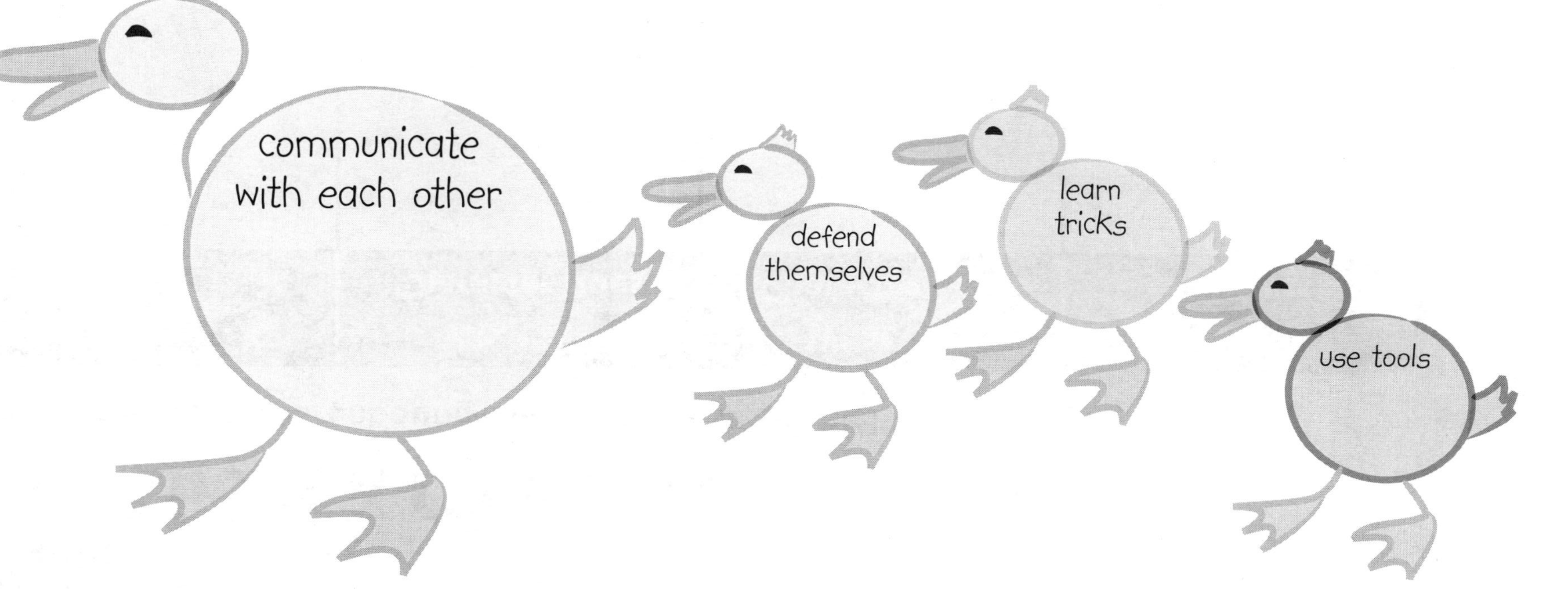

Tell About a Character

Make a character chart about a character in a story you have read.

Character	What the Character Does	What the Character Says	What It Shows

Tell a partner about your character and his or her traits.

PM2.2

Unit 2 | Animal Intelligence

Sentence Race

1. As a team, take 5 minutes to write as many sentences as you can using words in the chart. Each sentence must have a compound predicate. Use the words *and* and *or*.
2. Score 1 point for each sentence your team writes correctly.
3. Score an additional point for using more than 12 words from the chart in your sentences.
4. When time is up, check your sentences and add up your points. The team with the most points wins.

Animals	Verbs
leopard / leopards	eats / eat
spider / spiders	swings / swing
parakeet / parakeets	catches / catch
chipmunk / chipmunks	chirps / chirp
woodpecker / woodpeckers	reaches / reach
baboon / baboons	snoozes / snooze
horse / horses	climbs / climb
giraffe / giraffes	swallows / swallow

Edit and Proofread

Choose the Editing and Proofreading Marks you need to correct the passage. Look for the following:

- correct subject-verb agreement with compound subjects and compound predicates
- correct end punctuation

Editing and Proofreading Marks

∧	Add.
℘	Take out.
⊂⊃ ∧	Move to here.
∧ (comma)	Add comma.
⊙	Add period.

The African Gray parrot is my favorite bird. My next-door neighbor has one named Mr. Einstein. Cousin Rina and I visits him as often as we can. Sometimes we feeds and play with him for hours. He can be very funny!

African Grays are pretty noisy Mr. Einstein scream and whistles. African Gray parrots are also quite smart. Rina and my neighbor teaches Mr. Einstein a new word every week. Mr. Einstein speak and sings in Spanish, too. Rina laughs and wonder if he could learn to read!

When the doorbell rings, Mr. Einstein whistles or says, "Who is it?" Some visitors answers or laugh when they find out that a bird answered the door.

Read Directions Carefully

**Directions: Read each question about "Love and Roast Chicken."
Choose the best answer.**

Sample

> **1** Read the sentences. Which sentence tells about a
> character's traits? Circle the letter of the correct answer.
>
> Ⓐ Cuy lives on a farm.
>
> Ⓑ The farmer has a daughter named Florinda.
>
> ● Cuy plays tricks and tells a lot of stories.
>
> Ⓓ Tío Antonio is a fox, not a guinea pig.

2 Read. Choose the sentence that tells what happens last.

Ⓐ The farmer ties up Cuy.

Ⓑ The farmer says Cuy can help in the field.

Ⓒ The farmer laughs.

Ⓓ The farmer makes a sticky doll.

3 Choose the answer that best completes the sentence.
Cuy needs to hide from Tío Antonio, so he __________ .

Ⓐ works in the farmer's field

Ⓑ eats the alfalfa

Ⓒ makes a sticky doll

Ⓓ marries the farmer's daughter

 **Tell a partner how you used the test-taking strategy to
answer the question.**

          Unit 2 | Animal Intelligence

"Love and Roast Chicken"

Fill in what the character says and does. Write what this shows about the character.

Character Chart

Character	What the Character Does	What the Character Says	What It Shows
Cuy			
Tio Antonio			
the farmer			

"Love and Roast Chicken"

Expression in reading is how you use your voice to express feeling. Use this passage to practice reading with proper expression.

"*¡Qué tramposo!* What a rascal! You're not a farmworker,	9
you're a guinea pig!" cried the farmer. "And you've been eating	20
all my alfalfa! Well, Florinda loves to eat roast guinea pig,	31
and tomorrow we will eat YOU!"	37
He pulled Cuy free from the sticky gum doll. Then he tied him	50
to the eucalyptus tree and went back to bed.	59
"It can't get any worse than this!" thought Cuy. But here came	71
Tío Antonio sneaking toward the chicken coop.	78

From "Love and Roast Chicken," page 90.

Expression

1. ☐ Changes voice to match all the content.
2. ☐ Changes voice to match some of the content.
3. ☐ Changes voice, but it does not match content.
4. ☐ Does not change voice.

Accuracy and Rate Formula
Use the formula to measure a reader's accuracy and rate while reading aloud.

$$\underline{\hspace{3cm}} - \underline{\hspace{3cm}} = \underline{\hspace{3cm}}$$

words attempted in one minute	number of errors	words correct per minute (wcpm)

Animal Play

Grammar Rules: Compounds

A **compound subject** has two or more nouns. • When the subjects are joined by *or*, the verb matches the last subject. • When subjects are joined by *and*, the verb is plural.	John or Jen <u>feed</u> the dog once a day. (singular) Their mom or younger <u>brothers</u> <u>feed</u> the dog when they are gone. (plural) The <u>dog and cat</u> <u>are</u> happy to play together. (plural)
A **compound predicate** has two or more verbs with the same subject. • Subject and verbs match.	My <u>cat</u> <u>sleeps</u> and <u>plays</u>. (singular) The <u>Kittens</u> <u>run</u> and <u>jump</u> all day. (plural)

Read each sentence. Circle the correct verb in each item.

1. Hippos (teach/teaches) and (help/helps) their babies to swim.
2. My llama (romp/romps) and (chase/chases) my dog.
3. Dogs or cats (is/are) the most popular pets.
4. My brothers or sister (want/wants) a horse by next year.
5. My dog and cats (play/plays) together all the time.

 **Make a list of your five favorite animals. Take turns making sentences with compound subjects and predicates.**

Unit 2 | Animal Intelligence

That's a Negative

1. Cut apart the negative word cards and the subject/verb cards.

2. Place the subject/verb cards face up. Each player takes a negative word card and holds it so the others cannot see what it says.

3. Player 1 chooses a subject/verb card and then tries to make a negative sentence using the words on the cards. If a logical sentence cannot be made, the subject/verb card should go back on the table.

4. Play continues around the group.

no	no one
not	nobody
none	nothing
never	nowhere
we / see	I / travel
they / see	you / find
monkeys / swing	dog / sniffs
parakeet / chirps	elephant / sprays

You Said It!

1. Player 1 says a sentence about an animal and then asks, "What did I say?"

2. Players 2 and 3 write the sentence as a quotation, including the speaker's name and correct punctuation. Then, they proofread their sentences to make sure they used quotation marks, commas, and periods in the right places.

3. Players 2 and 3 display their written sentences. If a quotation is written correctly, Player 1 says, "You said it!"

4. If a quotation has a punctuation mistake, the team works together to correct it.

5. Play continues with players taking turns as Player 1, 2, and 3 until each player has said two sentences.

Compare Characters' Adventures

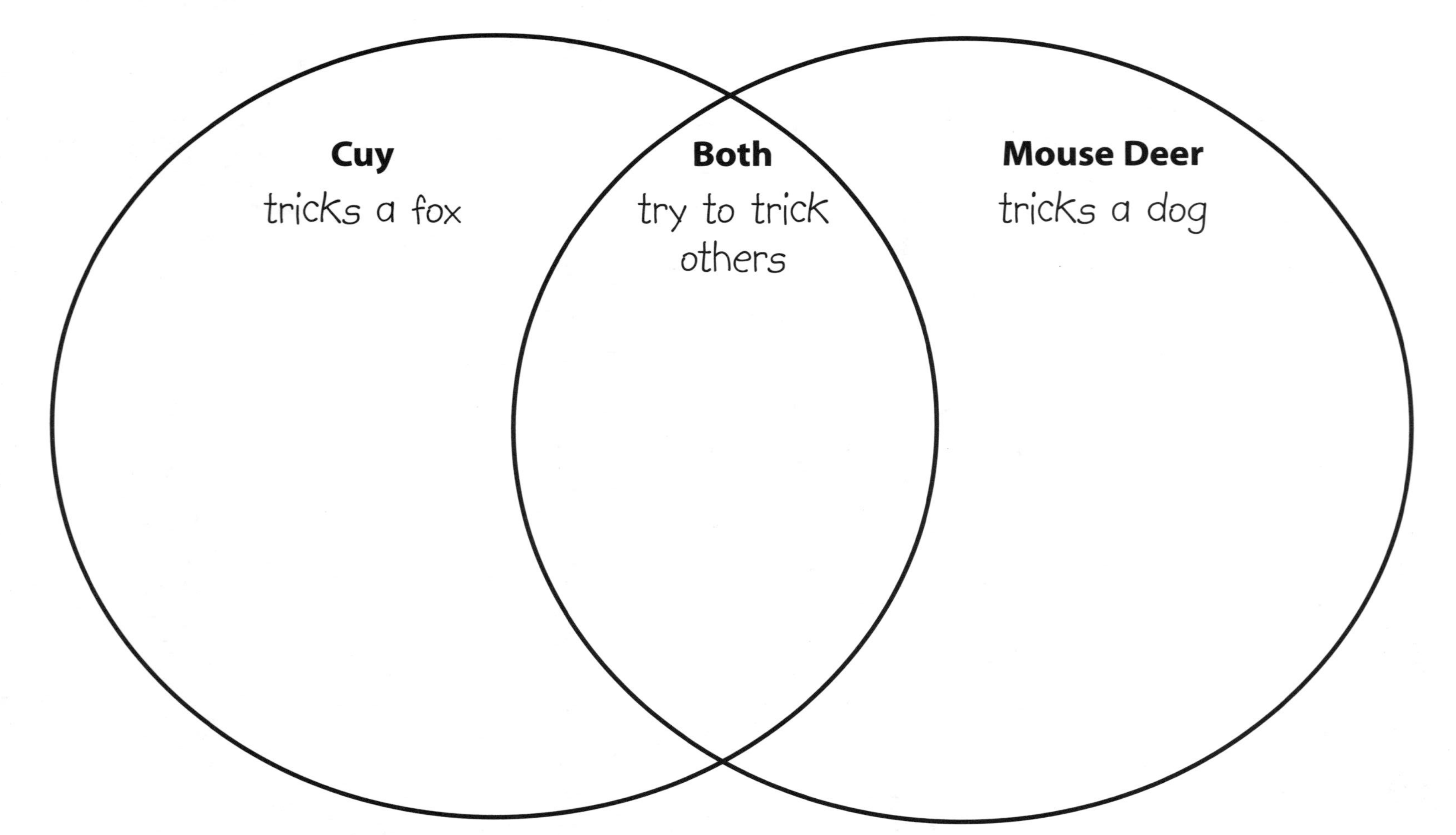

Use your Venn diagram to describe one character or both characters. Have your partner name the character or characters you describe. Then switch roles.

It's Not So Tricky!

Grammar Rules Kinds of Sentences

There are four kinds of sentences.

Name	Definition	Example
Statement	tells something	Mouse Deer is smart.
Question	asks something	Where is Mouse Deer?
Exclamation	shows strong feeling	What a trick!
Command	tells you to do something	Bring me some food. Be careful!

Name each sentence. Then write each sentence correctly.

1. where does Mouse Deer go

Question: Where does Mouse Deer go?

____

2. he is in the garden

____

3. what a big mistake

____

4. tell Mouse Deer to run

____

**Tell a partner what you know about trickster tales.
Use different kinds of sentences.**

How Pan Caused Panic

When the wind howled in the trees, ancient Greeks heard the voice of the god Pan, a half-human creature who thought it was funny to scare people.

One night, a man named Nicos walked alone through a windy forest. Pan was bored, but when he saw Nicos coming, he decided it would be fun to trick him. Pan took a deep breath and howled, "Wooooooooooo-eeeeeeee!" Nicos's heart pounded with terror as he ran screaming through the forest. Pan's howls soon turned to laughter. What fun it was to trick people!

Theme: Entertainment can sometimes hurt others.

Fox and Coyote

A favorite Native American trickster tale is about two clever animals, Fox and Coyote. One evening Fox was sitting by a lake. Suddenly, Coyote jumped out of the bushes and snarled, "I'm going to eat you!"

The moon reflected in the lake looked like a piece of cheese and Fox knew he needed to outsmart Coyote. So he said, "If you drink the lake, you can eat that piece of cheese."

Coyote began guzzling water from the lake. Soon his stomach ached. "I'll never drink it all!" he moaned.

"I'll get help," said Fox as he ran away. But, of course, he never came back!

Theme: Cleverness can get you out of trouble.

Anansi, the Spider

In this West African tale, Anansi, the clever spider, was jealous because people loved to tell stories about Nyame, the sky god. Anansi went to Nyame and said, "I want stories about me instead!"

Nyame replied, "To prove yourself, bring me a swarm of bees, a live python, and the King of the Forest."

First, Anansi walked among the trees carrying a huge gourd with a lid. The bees asked Anansi about the gourd. Anansi replied, "My silly friend says a swarm of bees can't fit in this gourd."

The bees laughed. "We can easily fit! We'll show you." Then the bees flew into the gourd.

Next, Anansi dragged a long stick behind him. The python slithered by and asked about the stick. Anansi explained, "My foolish friend says this stick is longer than a python."

"No way!" exclaimed the python. "I am the longest snake in the world!"

"I must tie you to the stick to measure correctly!" said Anansi.

Finally Anansi dug a huge pit and covered it with sticks and leaves. Leopard, the King of the Forest, walked by and fell right in!

Anansi brought Leopard, the python, and the bees to Nyame. "You have done the impossible!" cried Nyame. "From now on, all stories belong to clever Anansi the Spider."

Theme: Cleverness can get you what you want.

Comparison:

Topics: _______________________________________

Themes: ______________________________________

Events: _______________________________________

____

Edit and Proofread

Choose the Editing and Proofreading Marks you need to correct the passage. Look for correct usage of the following:

- correct negative sentences
- correct punctuation of quotations
- correct end punctuation

Editing and Proofreading Marks

∧	Add.
ℐ	Take out.
⟨?⟩	Add question mark.
⟨!⟩	Add exclamation mark.
⋀	Add comma.
⊙	Add period.
⋀	Add quotation mark.

When we brought our kitten home, he did not want ~~no~~ food. He just wanted us to pet him. Then my sister said "Come and see. He is he eating some kitten food" We all felt better?

Now he knows how to play catch. I have so much fun playing with him I throw a little crumpled paper ball. He catches it with his front paws. Nobody plays no other games with him. He and I just play catch. He makes me laugh.

"When you are older, I tell him, I will try to teach you to sit." I do not know if it will work, though. Can cats learn to sit. Even if my kitten just learns to snuggle on my lap, I'll be happy.

Take the Test

Grammar Rules: Punctuation

Negative sentences use words such as *no, not, never, none,* and *nowhere.* • Use only one negative word in a sentence.	**OK:** I am <u>not</u> taking the test today. **Not OK:** I am <u>not</u> taking <u>no</u> test today.
Use **commas** to precede, follow, or interrupt a quotation from a speaker. **Question** and **exclamation marks** should be inside quotation marks.	Mya asked, "Do we have a test today?" "Do we have a test today, or is it tomorrow?" Mya asked. "I studied so hard for the test!" said Mya.

Read the sentences. Place the quotation marks and the punctuation such as commas, question marks, and exclamation marks in the correct place.

1. You need to study said my mom, or you can't play football.

2. Do you know where my math book is I asked my sister.

3. Jenna answered It is over by the television.

4. Jenna said, I will help you study I love math!

5. Thank you, I said I need some extra help.

Talk to a partner. Write down everything your partner says. Place the quotation marks and end punctuation in the correct places.

Identify Main Idea and Details

Complete a main idea diagram about the kinds of commands that dogs follow.

Main Idea: Dogs can follow many different commands.

Detail: 1.

Detail: 2.

Detail: 3.

Coordination

1. Partner 1 says an independent clause about an animal.

2. Partner 2 spins the spinner, uses the conjunction to add another independent clause to the first clause, and says the new sentence aloud.

3. If Partner 1 agrees that the new sentence makes sense, Partner 2 begins his or her turn. If not, Partner 2 tries again.

4. After partners have played the game for five turns, each student chooses and writes his or her favorite two sentences, using correct punctuation.

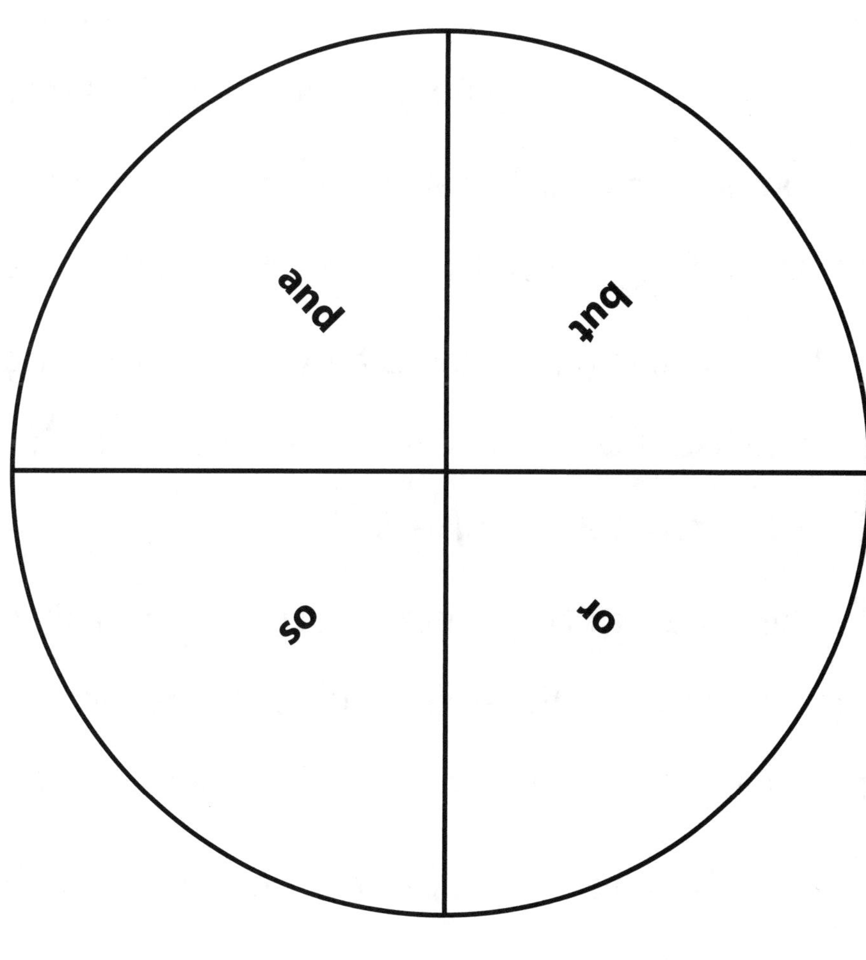

Make a Spinner

1. Put a paper clip over the center of the circle.
2. Push the point of a pencil into the paper, through the loop of the paper clip.
3. Spin the paper clip to play.

Edit and Proofread

Choose the editing and proofreading marks you need to correct the passage. Look for the following:

- run-on sentences
- correct coordinating conjunctions

Editing and Proofreading Marks

∧	Add.
ℒ	Take out.
⟳∧	Move to here.
∧,	Add comma.
⊙	Add period.

Fish Behaviors I Have Observed

You probably think that aquarium fish are all the same. I will tell you about my fish *so* you can learn how different they are.

I have two large fish tanks they both have African cichlids. In one I have cichlids from Lake Malawi, so the other tank has different cichlids. They are from Lake Tanganyika.

The larger cichlids sometimes chase the smaller fish. I have many rocks in the tanks the smaller fish can hide there. Other times, lots of the fish crowd together and then the larger fish won't pick on them.

Cichlids are very good parents. Are you surprised do you not believe it is true? Well, mother cichlids often carry eggs in their mouths they sometimes keep the babies there to protect them from other fish.

Test-Taking Strategy Practice

Read the question about "Animal Smarts." Choose the best answer.

Sample

> **1** What did Jane Goodall observe chimpanzees do in the wild? Circle the correct answer.
>
> - Ⓐ learn to speak
> - ● use tools
> - Ⓒ trick humans
> - Ⓓ count objects

2 Scientists can tell Koko the gorilla can think on her own because she __________ .

- Ⓐ knows more than 1,000 signs
- Ⓑ can make up new signs
- Ⓒ answers in sign language
- Ⓓ can communicate

3 Read the question. Write your answer in the space provided. How do meerkats communicate with each other?

____

____

____

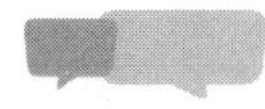 **Tell a partner how you used the strategy to answer the questions.**

For use with TE p. T128   **PM2.20**   **Unit 2** | Animal Intelligence

Name _________________________________ Date _______________

"Animal Smarts"

Make a Main Idea Diagram for "Animal Smarts."

Main Idea: Animals are __________ .

Detail:

Detail:

Detail:

Detail:

Detail:

Detail:

Detail:

 **Use your main idea diagram to explain the selection to a partner.**

PM2.21

"Animal Smarts"

Use this passage to practice reading with proper intonation.

To play a trick on someone may take some intelligence, too.   11

You have to guess how the person will act. Then you have   23

to find a way to trick the person. Some animals have been   35

terrific tricksters.   37

An orangutan named Fu Manchu tricked the zookeepers   45

at the Omaha Zoo. He escaped from his home three times.   56

First, he traded food with another orangutan for a piece of wire.   68

Then he hid the wire in his mouth. Finally, he used the wire to   82

pick the lock and set himself free!   89

From "Animal Smarts," page 122

Expression

1 ☐ Does not change pitch.   3 ☐ Changes pitch to match some of the content.

2 ☐ Changes pitch, but does not match content.   4 ☐ Changes pitch to match all of the content.

Accuracy and Rate Formula
Use the formula to measure a reader's accuracy and rate while reading aloud.

| _____________ | − | _____________ | = | _____________ |
| words attempted in one minute | | number of errors | | words correct per minute (wcpm) |

Pets

Grammar Rules: Clauses

An **independent clause** has a subject and a predicate. Independent clauses can be joined by a comma and the word *and, but, or,* and *so.*	<u>Full breed dogs</u> <u>are</u> <u>wonderful pets.</u> Full breed dogs are wonderful pets, but mutts are very loving
A **run-on sentence** is made up of two or more independent clauses that are not joined correctly.	**Not OK:** Full breed dogs are wonderful mutts are very loving. **OK:** Full breed dogs are wonderful, and mutts are very loving.

Read the sentences. Place a comma in the correct place and choose the correct conjunction that joins the independent clauses.

1. My mom works long hours (so/but) she is tired when she comes home.
2. I don't have a pet (and/but) my parents said I might get one.
3. Their dog misses them when they go away (and/so) they take it with them on trips.
4. My brother is allergic to cats (and/so) he sneezes when they are around.
5. We went to the pet store for a puppy (or/but) we got a bird.

With a partner, generate sentences from independent clauses using *and, but, or,* and *so.*

Big Break!

To Prepare:

1. Arrange your group into Team 1 and Team 2, each with a copy of this practice master.

2. Each team cuts out the words and sentences.

To Play:

1. Team 1 chooses and holds up one sentence strip. Team 2 follows by holding up the same sentence.

2. Both teams (1) cut the sentence into clauses, (2) choose the appropriate conjunction, and (3) place the comma between the clauses.

3. When both teams are ready, read aloud the new sentence together.

4. The game ends when all four sentences have been recreated.

The sparrows use the birdhouse all year they are protected.

Jaleel trains his puppy to stay I train my puppy, too.

Many butterflies come into our yard I don't catch them.

The lizard crawls on the rocks sometimes it scoots up the wall.

| and | so | or | but | , |

Grammar: Game

Complex Animals

To Prepare:

1. Each partner writes an independent clause and a dependent clause in the appropriate column.

2. Player 1 tosses one game marker onto each column.

3. Player 2 puts the clauses together to form a complex sentence and reads the sentence aloud.

4. Is the sentence silly? If it is, replace one clause with one that makes sense. Be careful! Did you write a complex sentence?

Independent Clauses	Dependent Clauses
Most owls hunt at night	because he is looking for bugs
Our hamster gets very excited	while other birds are sleeping
That woodpecker taps on my windowsill each morning	as they wiggle around in the pond
We watch tadpoles in the spring	when we give her peanut butter

Remember: A complex sentence must have one independent clause and at least one dependent clause.

Comparison Chart

Compare Facts

Put a check mark next to each fact if you find it in the article. Find more facts and write them on your chart.

Fact	Animal Smarts	The Clever Chimps of Fongoli
Chimps walk on the ground.	✓	✓
Rainforest chimps live in trees.		✓
Chimps eat insects.		
Some chimps eat bush babies.		
In 1960, Jane Goodall made a discovery about chimps.		
Chimps use tools.		

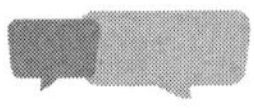 **Take turns with a partner. Ask each other questions about the facts provided in the two science articles.**

     PM2.26   Unit 2 | Animal Intelligence

What's the Combination?

Grammar Rules Combining Sentences

1. **Compound Sentence:** Join two independent clauses with a conjunction like *and, or,* or *but.* Use a comma before the conjunction.

   My dog learns new tricks, but my cat is too lazy.

2. **Complex Sentence:** Join a dependent clause and an independent clause with a conjunction like *because* or *when.* Use a comma when needed.

   Because dogs learn words, they respond to commands.

Underline conjunctions. Circle commas that separate ideas.

When my cousin came to visit, we went to the aquarium.

I learned about many water animals. My cousin liked the sharks, but

I liked the octopus. When I saw the octopus go through a maze,

I knew it had a good memory. When the octopus first tried the

maze, it made mistakes. Because it learned the way, it never makes

mistakes now. Now aquarium workers are teaching her different

shapes. I like this octopus, and even my cousin was impressed.

 **Write a compound sentence and a complex sentence to add to the story. Read them to a partner.**

Mark-Up Reading

Which Pet is Right for You?
by Michael Peska

Question: I want a pet that can learn tricks. What should I get?

Answer: A dog might be a good fit for you because dogs are clever. Some dogs have learned more than 100 tricks and commands! However, a parrot might be a better fit for you. Like dogs, parrots are very bright. But parrots can learn to speak words from human languages, which dogs can't do.

▲ Some dogs can do amazing tricks!

Like dogs, cats are fine pets as companions. On the other hand, if you want to teach your pet tricks, a cat might not be a good choice. Cats seem to have little interest in learning commands. Unlike cats, dogs seem eager to learn commands. So, a dog would probably enjoy learning tricks from you.

Similarity Signal Words	Similarity Statements
Like	<u>Like</u> dogs, parrots are very bright.
Difference Signal Words	**Difference Statements**
However	<u>However</u>, a parrot might be a better fit for you.

Which Pet is Right for You? (continued)

Question: We want to have our pet for a long time. What kinds of pets live the longest?

Answer: If you are looking for a pet that will live a long time, mice or hamsters would not be good choices. These animals have life spans of only two or three years. A cat, dog, or parrot would be a great choice, though. Cats and dogs typically live between ten and twenty years. Similarly, parrots can live fifty years or more! So before buying such a pet, be sure that you are committed to caring for your new friend for years to come.

▲ Some parrots live to be 50 years old!

Similarity Signal Words	Similarity Statements
Difference Signal Words	Difference Statements

Describe what you have learned about the structure of comparison writing.

____

____

____

____

____

Name ____ Date ________________

Edit and Proofread

Choose the Editing and Proofreading Marks you need to correct the passage. Look for correct usage of the following:

- run-on sentences
- complete sentences
- correct complex sentences
- correct compound sentences
- correct punctuation

Editing and Proofreading Marks

∧	Add.
ℐ	Take out.
/	Make lowercase.
∧,	Add comma.
⊙	Add period.

The platypus is the strangest animal. That I have ever seen. From the back it looks like a beaver or an otter from the front it is very different. It has a bill like a duck! Platypuses can swim underwater or they can run and dig on land.

Platypuses are mammals. Most mammals have live babies, platypuses lay eggs! The mother keeps the eggs warm. When the eggs hatch, the mother protects the babies they are very tiny.

A platypus hunts for food underwater. It pokes around the bottom for insects, shellfish, and worms, it scoops them up with its bill. When it hunts underwater. A platypus can hold its breath for more than a minute.

No matter what you think, a platypus is a unique animal.

Unit 2 | Animal Intelligence

Reteach: Grammar:

More Pets

Grammar Rules: Sentences

A **compound sentence** is made up of two or more **independent clauses**. The ideas are connected with the words *and, but, or,* and *so.*	OK: I keep saltwater fish, and I enjoy taking care of them. Not OK: I like saltwater fish, but my brother.
A **dependent clause** begins with words such as *if, because, since,* or *before.* A **complex sentence** has independent and dependent clauses.	If I seem unhappy, I miss my dog because she ran away.

Read the sentences. Write compound or complex on the line after each sentence.

1. Before I get a puppy, I research different breeds. ______________
2. I want a poodle, so I start saving my money. ______________
3. My mom said I have to be responsible with a dog, since dogs are hard work. ______________
4. We bought my poodle at the pet store, and we named him Sparky. ______________
5. We watch Sparky closely because he is small. ______________

 **With a partner, talk about pets using compound and complex sentences.**

For use with TE p. T145

Unit Concept Map

Amazing Places

Make a concept map with the answers to the Big Question: Why learn about other places?

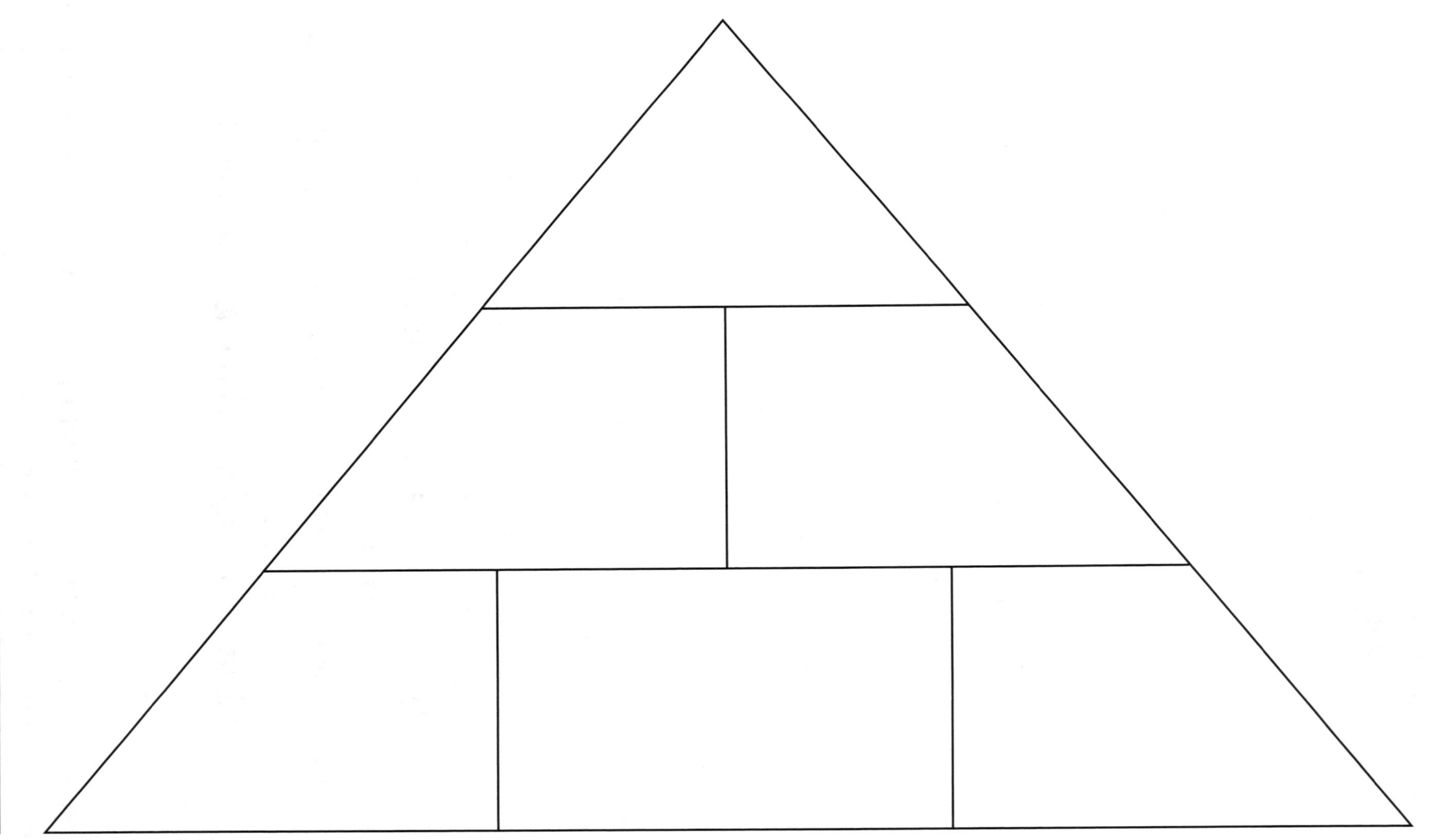

PM3.1

Theme Chart

Story Theme

Make a theme chart about a story you know.

Title	Characters
Setting	**Plot**

Theme (center oval)

 **Use your theme chart to tell a partner about the book.**

Grammar: Game

Word Cards

a	an	some
echo	mountains	horse
wishes	shelves	insect
oranges	blanket	monkey
hour	mango	adventure

For use with TE p. T143n

PM3.3

Edit and Proofread

Choose the Editing and Proofreading Marks you need to correct the passage. Look for the following:

- correct spelling of plural nouns
- correct use of *a, an, the, some*

Editing and Proofreading Marks

∧	Add.
ℒ	Take out.
⬭ ∧	Move to here.
∧,	Add comma.
⊙	Add period.

My parentes and I like to visit Badger Creek Nature Reserve near our town. It is an amazing place. Dozens of trails wind through the beautiful, thirty-acre reserve. The pathwaies are open 365 days an year, from dawn to dusk.

My favorite trail is one that passes through a area with a lot of bushs and trees. It's exciting to think that animals are hiding in burrows or among the branchees and leafs. Sometimes we catch an glimpse of them—raccoons, foxs, owls—even some snake.

We always walk quietly and speak in low voices, and we never pick any flowers, berrys, or other plants. After all, the purpose of the reserve is to protect a plants and animals!

Look for Important Words

Directions: Read each question about "How I Learned Geography." Choose the best answer.

Sample

1 What happens after the dad hangs up the map?

- Ⓐ The boy feels sad.
- ● The boy studies the map.
- Ⓒ The dad takes the map down.
- Ⓓ The dad buys the map.

2 Who was angry with the dad after he returned home?

- Ⓐ the boy and the couple
- Ⓑ the shopkeeper and the boy
- Ⓒ the mother and the couple
- Ⓓ the boy and his mother

3 What happened before the boy moved to the new country?

- Ⓐ The dad bought a map.
- Ⓑ He drew pictures.
- Ⓒ There was a war.
- Ⓓ He dreamed about far away places.

 **Tell a partner** how you used the strategy to answer the questions.

"How I Learned Geography"

Make a theme chart for "How I Learned Geography."

<table>
<tr><td>Title

"How I Learned Geography"</td><td>Characters</td></tr>
<tr><td>Setting</td><td>Theme

Plot
The family has to move because of war.</td></tr>
</table>

Use your theme chart to summarize the story and state the theme.

For use with TE p. T166a   **PM3.6**   **Unit 3** | Amazing Places

"How I Learned Geography"

Use this passage to practice reading with proper intonation.

It was nearly dark when he came home. He carried   10
a long roll of paper under his arm.   18

"I bought a map," he announced triumphantly.   25

"Where is the bread?" Mother asked.   31

"I bought a map," he said again.   38

Mother and I said nothing.   43

"I had enough money to buy only a tiny piece of bread,   55
and we would still be hungry," he explained apologetically.   64

"No supper tonight," Mother said bitterly. "We'll have   72
the map instead."   75

From "How I Learned Geography," page 158

Intonation

| 1 ☐ Does not change pitch. | 3 ☐ Changes pitch to match some of the content. |
| 2 ☐ Changes pitch, but does not match content. | 4 ☐ Changes pitch to match all of the content. |

Accuracy and Rate Formula
Use the formula to measure a reader's accuracy and rate while reading aloud.

_______ − _______ = _______
words attempted   number of errors   words correct per minute
in one minute   (wcpm)

Lucky Dogs

Grammar Rules: Nouns

A **noun** names a person or thing. • To make most nouns plural, add -*s* to the end. • Some nouns change their spelling for plurals	Ana has two dog<u>s</u>. They love to roll in the lea<u>ves</u>.
The articles *a, an, the,* and *some* signal a noun. • Use *a* or *an* before most singular nouns. • Use *some* with a plural noun. • Use *the* with both singular and plural nouns.	One dog likes to chew <u>a</u> bone. The other dog likes to play with <u>an</u> apple. The dogs love to play with <u>some</u> toys. <u>The</u> toys make them happy.

Circle the word that completes each sentence.

1. Ana wants four more (pet/pets).
2. She gives her pets good (lives/lifes).
3. Ana will give them (some/a) treats each day.
4. They can play with (the/a) toys she has.
5. (A/An) new pet is fun, so four will be even more fun.

Tell a partner about three things you can give a pet to make it happy. Use nouns and articles to tell these things.

Daily Grammar: Game
This or That

Demonstrative Adjectives

- Use **this** or **that** before one person, place, or thing.

This palm tree is growing on the beach.

That building looks very old.

Turn to pages 144–145 in the Anthology and use the sentences above to describe the objects in the photograph. Then, play a game using more pictures in the book.

1. Team One holds the book, finds a picture, points to it, and describes something in the image using *this*.

2. Team Two points to the picture in Team One's hands and uses *that* to add more description.

3. Team Two takes the book, points to another picture, and describes the image using *this*.

4. Team One points to the picture in Team Two's hands and uses *that* to add more description.

5. Continue trading the book back and forth for three more rounds. Use *this* when your team has the book. Use *that* when the other team has the book.

These or Those

Demonstrative Adjectives

- Use **these** or **those** before more than one person, place, or thing.

These people near us are working hard.

Those people over there are coming to help.

Turn to page 195 in the Anthology and use the sentences above to describe the people you see in the photograph. Then, play a game using more pictures in your book.

1. Team One holds the book, finds a picture, points to it, and describes something in the image using *these.*

2. Team Two points to the picture in Team One's hands and uses *those* to add more description.

3. Team Two takes the book, points to another picture, and describes the image using *these.*

4. Team One points to the picture in Team Two's hands and uses *those* to add more description.

5. Continue trading the book back and forth for three more rounds. Use *these* when your team has the book. Use *those* when the other team has the book.

Compare Figurative Language

Write the figurative language you find in the story and the poem.
Label each type of figurative language.

"How I Learned Geography"	"Tortillas Like Africa"
"icy winds licked my face" (personification)	"Here was Chile, thin as a tie." (simile)

 **Take turns with a partner. Tell how each metaphor or simile helps you picture what is happening.**

Grammar: Practice

Moving Day

Plural Nouns

1. To make many nouns plural, add -s to the end.

   land → lands

2. For nouns that end in *x, ch, sh, s, z,* and sometimes *o,* add -es.

   bench → benches   volcano → volcanoes

3. For nouns that end in *y,* change the *y* to *i* and add -es.
   For nouns that end with a vowel then *y,* just add -s.

   lady → ladies   way → ways

Write the plural nouns.

I looked around at our new home. The floor was covered

in ___*boxes*___ . My mother was unpacking _________ in the kitchen.
   (box)   (glass)

In three _________ I started school. I wondered if my _________
        (day)   (class)

would be hard. I wondered if these _________ played football. My
                                (boy)

two little _________ did not seem worried. Mama saw the look on
        (sister)

my face. She said there were other _________ from Mexico on our
                             (family)

block. She said some of the _________ were from other _________,
                 (coach)   (country)

too. I started to feel better about my new home.

Pick two plural nouns from above and write new sentences. Read them to a partner.

Mark-Up Reading

Travel
by Robert Louis Stevenson

I should like to rise and go

Where the golden apples grow;

Where below another sky

Parrot islands anchored lie,

And, watched by cockatoos and goats,

Lonely Crusoes building boats;

Where in sunshine reaching out

Eastern cities, miles about,

Are with **mosque and minaret**

Among the sandy gardens set,

And the rich goods from near and far

Hang for sale in the **bazaar**;

Where the Great Wall round China goes,

And on one side the desert blows,

And with bell and voice and drum,

Cities on the other hum;

Where are forests, hot as fire,

Wide as England, tall as a **spire**,

In Other Words

Lonely Crusoes people who are alone in
unusual places, like the character in the
story Robinson Crusoe

mosque and minaret the building where
people worship and the tall tower that is
part of that building

bazaar marketplace

spire tall, narrow tower on a roof; steeple

Travel (continued)

Where the knotty crocodile

Lies and blinks in the Nile,

And the red flamingo flies

Hunting fish before his eyes;

Where in jungles, near and far,

Man-**devouring** tigers are,

Lying close and giving ear

Lest the hunt be drawing near,

Or **a comer-by** be seen

Swinging in a **palanquin**;

Where among the desert sands

Some deserted city stands,

All its children, **sweep** and prince,

Growan to manhood **ages since**,

Not a foot in street or house,

Not a stir of child or mouse,

And when kindly falls the night,

In all the town no spark of light.

There I'll come when I'm a man

With a camel caravan;

Light a flower in the gloom

Of some dusty dining-room;

See the pictures on the walls,

Heroes, fights, and festivals;

And in a corner find the toys

Of the old Egyptian boys.

In Other Words

devouring eating

Lest In Case

a comer-by someone coming by

palanquin covered seat which is carried by other people

sweep working people, like chimney sweeps

ages since a long time ago

Edit and Proofread

Choose the Editing and Proofreading Marks you need to correct the passage. Look for:

- correct spelling of plural nouns
- correct use of *this, that, these, those*

Editing and Proofreading Marks

∧	Add.
ℐ	Take out.
⟳∧	Move to here.
∧̣	Add comma.
⊙	Add period.

Angelo showed me his photographs of Costa Rica. He had pictures of hoteles, forests, beachs—you name it! I put on my glassies.

I pointed to some monkeys. "What are these monkeys called?"

"That monkeys are called howlers," he said, "because they make really loud noisies."

Angelo pointed to a beautiful bird. "People say those bird is the most beautiful bird in the world. It is," he added.

"Did you see hummingbirdes?" I asked.

"Yes, I did!"

My friends have familys all over the place. I haven't been to other countrys. One day, I will travel and see the varietys of animals myself!

Chef Ramon

Grammar Rules: Adjectives

The words *this*, *that*, *these*, and *those* are **demonstrative adjectives** that show if a noun is near or far. They also show if a noun is singular or plural.

<u>This</u> sandwich in my hand is mine. (near, singular)

<u>Those</u> sandwiches on the table are Mary's. (far, plural)

To make most nouns plural, add -*s* to the end.

- Add -*es* to nouns that end in *x*, *ch*, *sh*, *ss*, *z*, and sometimes *o*.

Ramon makes lunch<u>es</u> for his family.

- Some nouns change their spelling for plurals.

He makes lunches for other famil<u>ies</u>.

Circle the word that correctly completes each sentence.

1. Ramon makes ten (boxes/boxs) of lunch every day.
2. He gathers his (supplys/supplies) early in the morning.
3. Ramon's (dayes/days) start with a lot of work.
4. He gives (this/these) lunches to his family.
5. (Those/That) sandwiches will be good to eat.

 **With a partner, role-play a conversation about making lunch with Ramon. Take turns using sentences with demonstrative adjectives and plural nouns.**

Logical Order

Write an outline of trips you have taken.

Outline

I. ____

    A. ____

    B. ____

II. ____

    A. ____

    B. ____

III. ____

    A. ____

    B. ____

 **Work with a partner. Take turns using your outline to tell about your trips.**

Name ____ Date _______________________

In a Box Game

Grammar Rules Collective Nouns

- A collective noun names a group of people, animals, or things.

committee

panel

tribe

1. Play with a partner.
2. Choose a box without initials in it. Read the word and decide whether it is a collective noun.
3. If your partner agrees that it is a collective noun, draw an X over the word. If your partner agrees that it is not a collective noun, draw a circle around the word. Then write your initials on the line in the box.
4. When all boxes are taken, your boxes. The player with the most boxes is the winner.

staff	traveler	band	pack
________	________	________	________
photographer	herd	audience	area
________	________	________	________
team	class	neighbor	home
________	________	________	________
flock	crowd	leader	community
________	________	________	________

For use with TE p. T173u

PM3.18

Daily Grammar: Grammar and Writing

Edit and Proofread

Choose the Editing and Proofreading Marks you need to correct the passage. Look for:

- correct use of collective nouns
- correct subject-verb agreement

Editing and Proofreading Marks

∧	Add.
℘	Take out.
⬭ ∧	Move to here.
∧,	Add comma.
⊙	Add period.

Our class are going to the new nature center tomorrow. Our class

donated money to help build it, so the school administration have

agreed to let us visit it on a school day. We're excited!

Since tomorrow is opening day, a crowd are likely to be there.

I hope we get to see everything. I love nature!

The nature center has many different areas. A flock of sheeps

graze in the south pasture. There are herds of goats and llamas in

the north pasture, and there are a warren of rabbits in the hollow.

Down by the lake, there are a gaggle of geese. Along one trail, a bee

colony are making honey, and an army of ants is creating a huge hill.

I hope our group visit them all.

Look for Important Words

Directions: Read each question about "Extreme Earth." Choose the best answer.

Sample

1 Which place has the hottest temperature on Earth?

Ⓐ The Great Barrier Reef

Ⓑ The Amazon

● The Sahara

Ⓓ Antarctica

2 Nomads move from place to place in the hot desert. How do they know when to move?

Ⓐ Sunlight bakes the ground.

Ⓑ There is no water or food.

Ⓒ The fennec adapts to life in the desert.

Ⓓ The animals run, walk, or crawl.

3 What happens after a polyp dies?

Ⓐ The skeleton protects the polyp's soft body.

Ⓑ Each polyp takes chemicals from the sea.

Ⓒ The polyp makes a hard outer skeleton.

Ⓓ New polyps build on the skeleton that is left.

 **How did you use the test-taking strategy to answer the question?**

Outline

Outline the main ideas and details in "Extreme Earth."

Outline

   I. Mount Everest is the tallest mountain on the planet.

      A. It is 8,850 meters above sea level.

      B. No plants or animals live there.

  II. The Sahara is the largest hot desert on Earth.

      A. Only 8 centimeters of rain fall each year.

      B. Few plants and animals live there.

 III. ____

      A. ____

      B. ____

 IV. ____

      A. ____

      B. ____

  V. ____

      A. ____

      B. ____

 VI. ____

 **Use your outline to summarize "Extreme Earth" with a partner. Include Key Words in your main ideas and details.**

Fluency Practice

"Extreme Earth"

Use this passage to practice reading with proper phrasing.

Our next extreme place is under water. It is the Great   11

Barrier Reef, off the coast of Australia. It is the largest reef on   24

Earth. It is bigger than New Mexico. In fact, the Great Barrier   36

Reef is the largest thing ever built by living creatures.   46

The builders are tiny animals called coral polyps. Each   55

polyp takes chemicals from the sea. It uses the chemicals to   66

make a hard outer skeleton shaped like a cup. This cup   77

protects the polyp's soft body.   82

From "Extreme Earth," page 188

Phrasing

| 1 | ☐ Rarely pauses while reading the text. | | 3 | ☐ Frequently pauses at appropriate points in the text. |

| 2 | ☐ Occasionally pauses while reading the text. | | 4 | ☐ Consistently pauses at all appropriate points in the text. |

Accuracy and Rate Formula

Use the formula to measure a reader's accuracy and rate while reading aloud.

__________ − __________ = __________
words attempted   number of errors   words correct per minute
in one minute   (wcpm)

A Group Trip

Grammar Rules: Nouns

A **collective noun** names a group of people, animals, or things.

- It is **singular** because it names **one** group of people, animals, or things. A collective noun always has a singular verb.

The <u>band</u> <u>plays</u> every day. A <u>crowd</u> <u>gathers</u> to listen. But an ant <u>colony</u> <u>is</u> biting people.

Use the correct form of the verb to complete each sentence. Then read the sentences to a partner.

1. Joel's family _____________ my family's best friends.
    (be)

2. The group _____________ planning a trip together.
    (be)

3. We will take a class in scuba diving. The class _____________ all day for two days to learn safety tips.
    (practice)

4. If a school of fish _____________ by, I will be excited.
    (swim)

5. Our community _____________ to see the photos from our trip.
    (want)

Tell a partner three things that a group can do together. Use collective nouns to tell about the activities.

Let's Get Specific

1. Cut out the circle below. Push the brad through the center. Open the band in the back. Hook a large paper clip over the brad to make a spinner.

2. Draw a 6-column chart. Write a different common noun from the spinner at the top of each column.

3. Spin the spinner.

4. Name a proper noun that goes with the common noun.

5. Write the proper noun under the correct heading. Have your partner check for correct capitalization.

6. Keep playing until each column has three proper nouns in it.

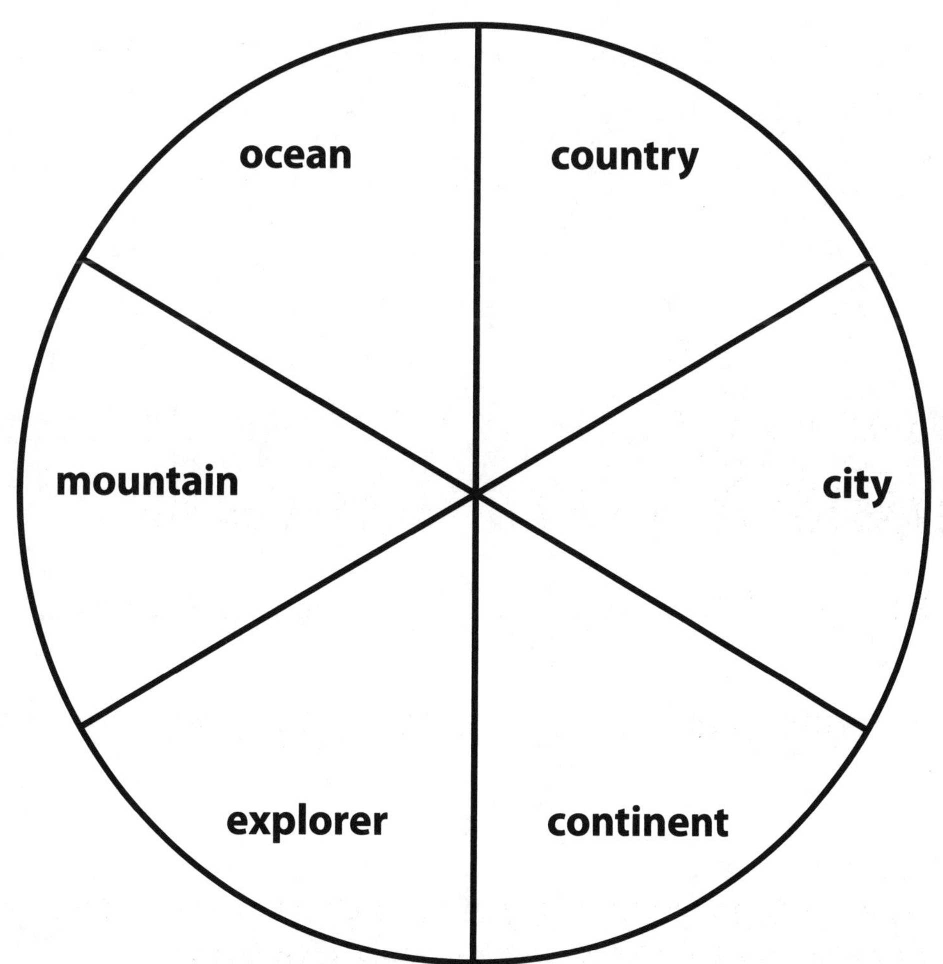

Grammar: Game

Let's Agree

Irregular Plural Nouns

- An **irregular noun** does not use **-s** or **-es** to form the plural.

woman → **women**
goose → **geese**
mouse → **mice**
foot → **feet**
child → **children**
person → **people**
ox → **oxen**
tooth → **teeth**

1. **Play with a partner.**

2. **Make a card for each word below. Place the cards face down. Take turns turning over a card.**

3. **Spell the plural form of each word and use it in a sentence. If your partner agrees, keep the card. The player with the most cards wins.**

woman	mouse	tooth	ox
goose	foot	child	person

For use with TE p. T197k   **PM3.25**   **Unit 3** | Amazing Places

Comparison Chart

Photographing the World

Write yes or no next to each feature. List more text features.

features	"Extreme Earth"	"Photographing the World"
1. title	yes	yes
2. section headings		
3. photographs		
4. captions		
5. maps		

 **Talk about features of the two genres with a partner. Each partner can describe one of the genres. Mention all features of your genre that you listed in the chart.**

Saving a Forest from Fire

Grammar Rules Irregular Plural Nouns

rule	example
Some plural nouns do not add -s or -es to show "more than one." They change their spelling.	*goose* → *geese*
Some nouns do not change at all when they become plural.	*moose* → *moose*

Write the plural form of the noun in the box to complete each sentence.

1. | deer | There are many _____deer_____ living in the forest. A

   fire put them in danger.

2. | fireman | It took forty __________ to put out the fire. They

   saved the animals and some very old trees.

3. | person | After the fire was out, many __________ offered to

   help.

4. | child | The town's __________ gathered food for the animals.

   Pick two of the plural nouns from above and write new sentences. Read them aloud to a partner.

Chile: Where Nature Goes to Extremes

by Nathan Sanchez

The country of Chile is a land of amazing physical extremes. You can see this in its shape, which looks like a ribbon. Chile is extremely long but very narrow. From its northern boundary with Peru to its southern tip at Cape Horn, Chile is 2,700 miles long. However, the country's average width is only 110 miles. At one point, Chile is only 9.6 miles wide!

Chile is bounded along its lengthy western coast by the Pacific Ocean. This long coastline accounts for more than one-half of South America's Pacific coast. Chile has 2,700 miles of sparkling ocean views. Located just a few miles inland from these shores, however, is the Atacama Desert, another example of Chile's extreme features. The Atacama Desert is the driest region on Earth. Scientists say that in some parts not one drop of rain has fallen in 120,000 years!

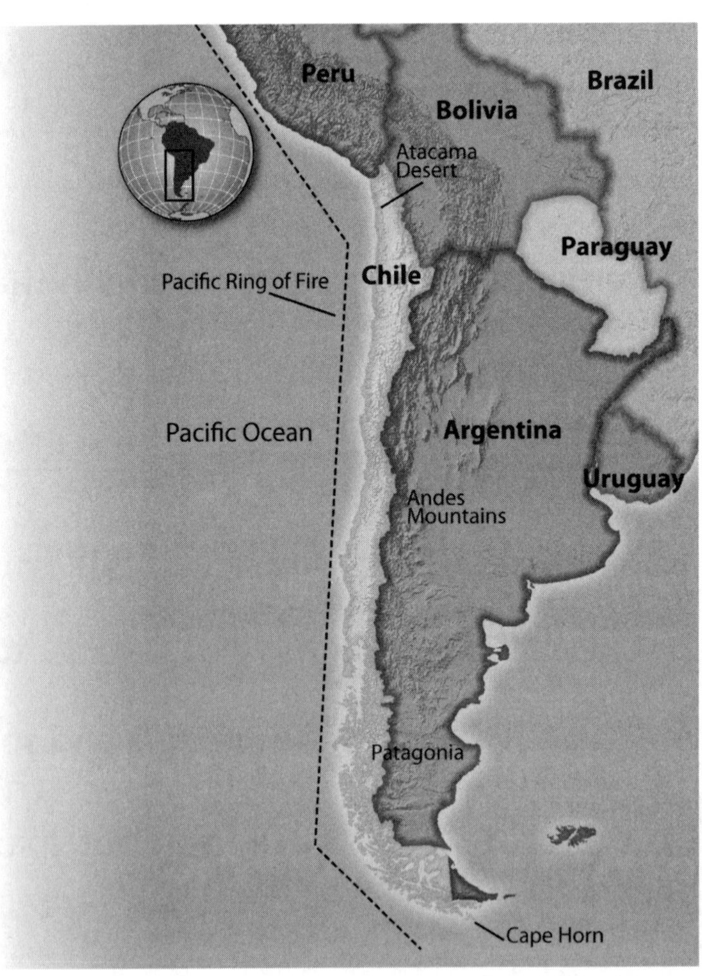

▲ Chile, Land of Extremes

Chile: Where Nature Goes to Extremes (continued)

Another example of Chile's natural extremes is the Andes mountain range. This is the world's longest continuous mountain chain. The high, rocky peaks of the Andes soar more than 22,000 feet. By contrast, at the

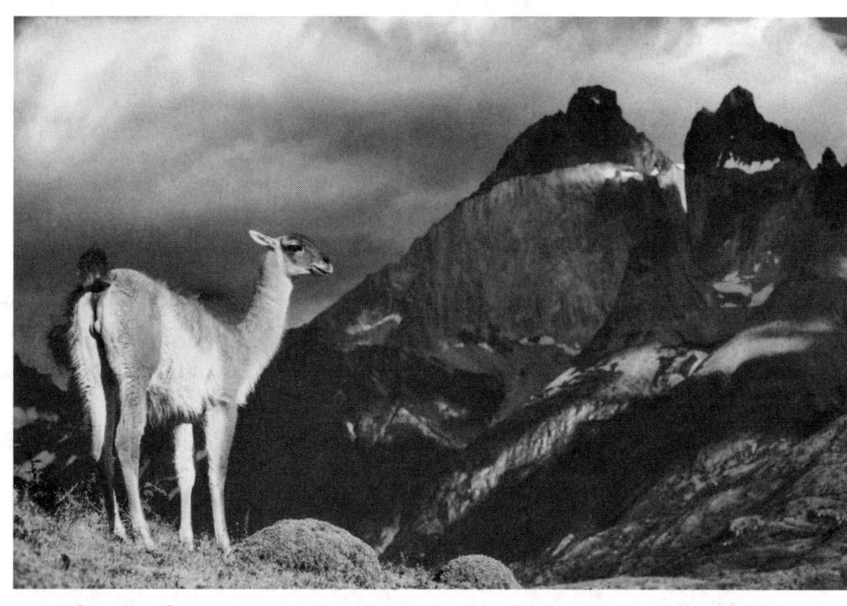

▲ The Andes mountain chain is the longest in the world.

base of the Andes sprawl the vast, flat ice fields of Patagonia. These are the second-largest ice fields in the world.

The shores of Chile are beautiful, but they are also located along the Pacific Ring of Fire, the meeting place of two of Earth's plates. When these pieces of Earth's crust shift, it creates earthquakes across the region. This is certainly the most dramatic and deadly way in which nature goes to extremes in Chile.

Explanation

....

....

....

....

Daily Grammar: Grammar and Writing

Edit and Proofread

Choose the Editing and Proofreading Marks you need to correct the passage. Look for:

- correct capitalization of common and proper nouns
- correct spelling of irregular plural nouns

Editing and Proofreading Marks

∧	Add.
✍	Take out.
≡	Make capital.
/	Make lower case.

Have you ever been to a national park? The united states has great ones!

My favorite is Bryce Canyon in utah. It's a Fairyland! For thousands of years, nature has carved the rocks into fanciful shapes. There are castles, ships, towers. My favorite Trail is named the fairyland loop trail.

I also love Denali national park. It's in alaska. Talk about different! Denali means "the high one" in the language of the athabascans, and is it ever! Denali is the highest mountain in north America, and it's covered with snows. You can see black bears, grizzlies, mooses, and sheeps. You might even see wolves or foxes.

Great Jobs

Grammar Rules: Nouns

• A **common noun** names any person, place, thing, or idea. It starts with a small letter.	A <u>firefighter</u> has an important job.
• A **proper noun** names a particular person, place, thing, or idea. It starts with a capital letter.	My friend <u>Roberto</u> is proud that his dad is a firefighter.
• Most nouns use –s or -es to show more than one. But an **irregular noun** does not use -s or -es to show more than one.	When I was a child, I wanted to be a firefighter. Most <u>children</u> I knew thought about it, too.

Complete these sentences by writing the correct word on the line.

1. My teacher, Mr. _____________, is a good teacher. (stanford/Stanford)
2. He tells us about many different _____________. (jobs/Jobs)
3. We can be an animal doctor and take care of _____________. (gooses/geese)
4. We can catch _____________ for a living. (fishes/fish)
5. We can cook _____________ in a restaurant. (deer/deers)

 With a partner, take turns and use irregular plural nouns to talk about different animals.

Name ___________________________   Date ___________________________

Unit Concept Map

Power of Nature

Make a concept map with the answers to the Big Question:
How do we relate to nature?

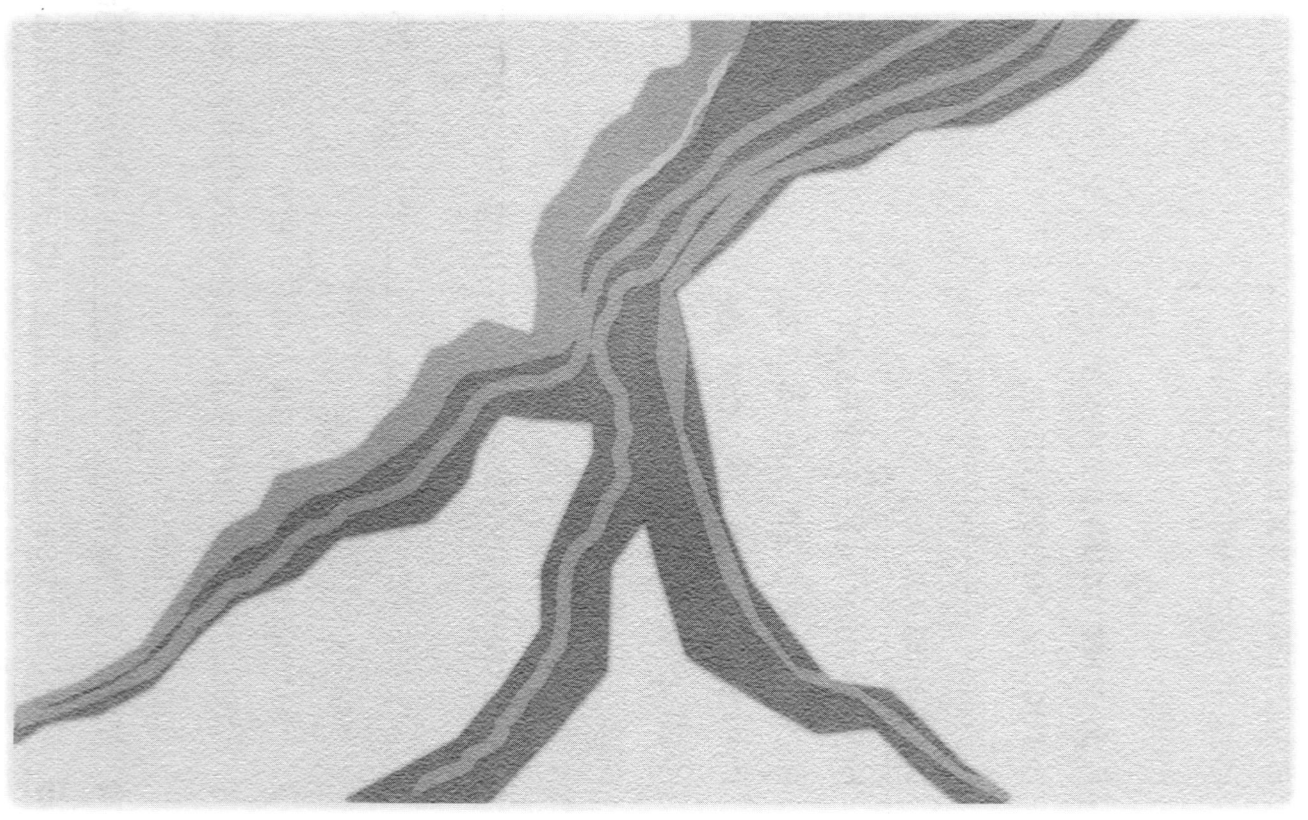

For use with TE p. T215

PM4.1

Cause-and-Effect Chart

What Happens to Soil?

Make a cause-and-effect chart to tell what can happen to soil and why.

Cause   **Effect**

 **Tell a partner about a cause-and-effect relationship. Use signal words such as** *because, since, so,* **and** *as a result.*

For use with TE p. T217a   **PM4.2**   **Unit 4** | Power of Nature

Grammar: Game

Agree with Me

Topics

SUN	HAIL	SNOW	WIND	RAIN

1. Cut out the cards and arrange them on a desk or the floor.

2. Toss a beanbag onto a gray helping verb card.

3. Toss another beanbag onto a subject card.

4. Toss a third beanbag onto a main verb card.

5. If the first two cards agree, choose topic from the box and orally compose a sentence. Be sure to use the subject, helping verb, and main verb in your sentence. If the subject and helping verb do not agree, choose a different helping verb. Then compose your sentence.

am		are		is
I	you	we		they
he		she		it
slipping	running	flying	pounding	blowing

Edit and Proofread

Choose the Editing and Proofreading Marks you need to correct the passage. Look for the following:

- spelling of present-tense verbs
- subject-verb agreement with forms of *be*
- present progressive

Editing and Proofreading Marks

∧	Add.
℘	Take out.
⟃⟄∧	Move to here.
⋏	Add comma.
⊙	Add period.

We lives in a part of the country with some very intense weather.

The mayor are scheduling community meetings four times a year to

make sure we are ready for anything. She am planning one next week.

Before the cold weather start, the meeting is about getting ready

for winter. The police chief reminds us to check our tires. He tell us to

have blankets in our cars, in case we am stuck in the snow.

In early spring, we hear about tornado safety I is always nervous

about this time of year because tornadoes are so unpredictable. The

summer meeting are about using sunscreen and conserving water.

Weather affect us every day, so it's important to be prepared. Our

town sure is!

Test-Taking Strategy Practice

Understand the Question

Directions: Read each question. Choose the best answer.

Sample

1 All of the following are caused by wind except __________?

- Ⓐ hurricanes
- ● rain
- Ⓒ tornadoes
- Ⓓ erosion

2 Where do wind farms work best?

- Ⓐ in wide-open spaces
- Ⓑ near a city
- Ⓒ in a forest
- Ⓓ in a thunderstorm

3 What are the most predictable winds that sailors used?

- Ⓐ warm rising air
- Ⓑ trade winds
- Ⓒ twisters
- Ⓓ hurricane winds

 **Tell a partner how you used the test-taking strategy to answer the questions.**

Name ____________________ Date ____________

Cause-and-Effect Chart

"Wind at Work"

Make a cause-and-effect chart for "Wind at Work."

Causes		Effects
Sunlight warms the land and the air above it.	→	The warm air rises.
Sunlight hits Earth most directly at the equator.	→	
	→	
	→	
	→	
	→	
	→	

Share your cause-and-effect chart with a partner. Work together to write sentences with the words *because, since, so,* and *as a result* to tell about each cause-and-effect relationship.

"Wind at Work"

Use this passage to practice reading with proper intonation.

Tornadoes may be terrifying, but hurricanes are huge and 9

terrifying. A hurricane can easily stretch across three states 18

with winds that pack a major punch. 25

Hurricanes form over tropical oceans. Warm, moist air rises. 34

More air moves in underneath and then rises. Big, wet clouds 45

start to gather. 48

Over a few days, Earth's rotation causes the growing mass 58

of clouds to spin. When winds reach 119 kilometers (74 miles) 69

an hour, the storm becomes a hurricane. 76

Once hurricanes hit land, they can do extreme damage. 85

The winds can destroy trees and buildings, and huge waves 95

flood coasts. 97

From "Wind at Work," page 234

Intonation

1 ☐ Does not change pitch.   3 ☐ Changes pitch to match some of the content.

2 ☐ Changes pitch, but does not match content.   4 ☐ Changes pitch to match all of the content.

Accuracy and Rate Formula

Use the formula to measure a reader's accuracy and rate while reading aloud.

___________	−	___________	=	___________
words attempted in one minute		number of errors		words correct per minute (wcpm)

Being Outside

Grammar Rules Verbs

Present Tense A verb in the **present tense** shows • that the action is happening now • that the action happens all the time	Some winds **blow** in regular patterns. Air **moves** around the Earth all the time.
Subject-Verb Agreement with *be* The **subject** and **verb** must agree, even when other words come between them.	Earth's **water is** a precious resource. **Rivers** around the world **are** important to all life.
Present-Progressive Form The **present-progressive** form tells about an action as it is happening.	Water is **flowing** both night and day. Winds are **blowing** constantly around the world.

Choose the correct form of each verb to complete the sentences.

1. Anne always _____________ (whisper) to her little brother.

2. She _____________ (carry) her lunch in a basket.

3. Anne's aunt _____________ (make) tortillas for the family.

4. They _____________ (be/eat) enchiladas.

5. Anne _____________ (think) the meal is delicious.

Have your partner silently act out a scene. Narrate the scene with correct subject-verb agreement.

Grammar: Game

What Is Happening Now?

1. Play with a partner.

2. Spin the spinner.

3. Change each sentence to make it present progressive.

Example:
He sails on the bay./ He is sailing on the bay.

Spinner wheel sections:
- We head to the town pool to cool off.
- Sprinklers splash the younger children.
- Ocean waves pound the shore.
- The lake shimmers in the sunlight.
- Firefighters in boats rescue people.
- Today's heavy rain floods the valley.

Make a Spinner

1. Put a paper clip over the center of the spinner.
2. Touch the point of a pencil on the middle of the wheel and through the loop of the paper clip.
3. Spin the paper clip to make a spinner.

Name _______________________   Date _______________

Action Verb Charades

1. Work in a group of four. Write each sentence below on a separate slip of paper.

2. Take turns picking a slip and acting out the action verb written on it. If the slip says "He/she," act out the action verb yourself. If it says "They," show the slip of paper to one group member. Act out the action verb together.

3. As you act, other group members guess what you are doing, using the sentence frames "He/she ____________." or "They ____________."

4. Once the correct action is guessed, all group members write the sentence.

5. Continue playing until all the actions have been completed.

They dance.	He/She throws.
He/She runs.	He/She catches.
He/She writes.	They talk.
They read.	They draw.
They skip.	He/She digs.
He/She spins.	They swim.
He/She climbs.	He/She plants.
They build.	He/She crawls.

Compare Genres

Compare a science article and a persuasive essay.

Topic	"Wind at Work"	"Water: The Blue Gold"
	wind	water
Point of view: first person or third person?	third person	
Author's purpose		
What statements from the text support the purpose?		
Does the author express a strong opinion about the topic? Give an example. Explain it.		
What did you learn?		

 **Take turns with a partner. Name other ways the selections are similar and different.**

Name ____ Date ___________________

Lots of Action

Grammar Rules Present-Tense Action Verbs

1. An action verb tells what the subject does.

2. The verb must agree with the subject.

he, she, it, or singular noun: add -*s* or -*es* to the verb	*I, you, we, they, or plural noun:* add nothing to the verb
Mom **tells** me to close the window.	I **listen to** the wind.
The rain **begins** to fall.	The leaves **blow** across the street.
The thunder **crashes** and **booms**.	The tree branches **bend**.

Imagine yourself in the middle of a storm. Use present-tense action verbs to tell what you, other people, and things do in the storm. Write your sentences. Example: When we hear thunder, Mom turns off the TV.

____

____

____

____

____

____

 **Read your sentences to a partner.**

Saving Giants

by Jason Chapman

Last summer my family and I visited the redwood forest in California. I learned so much about these magnificent trees. I believe that saving these forests is important because many living things, including people, depend on them. Only about 5% of the original redwood forests remain. The redwood forests are scarce resources that we must protect.

Redwoods are extraordinary living things we should care for. What makes these trees so special? First, they can live for more than 1,500 years. Also, they aren't just big— they're colossal! Some even grow to heights of more than 300 feet. That's as tall as the Statue of Liberty! If we don't work hard to save these forests now, future generations might never get to see these amazing natural skyscrapers.

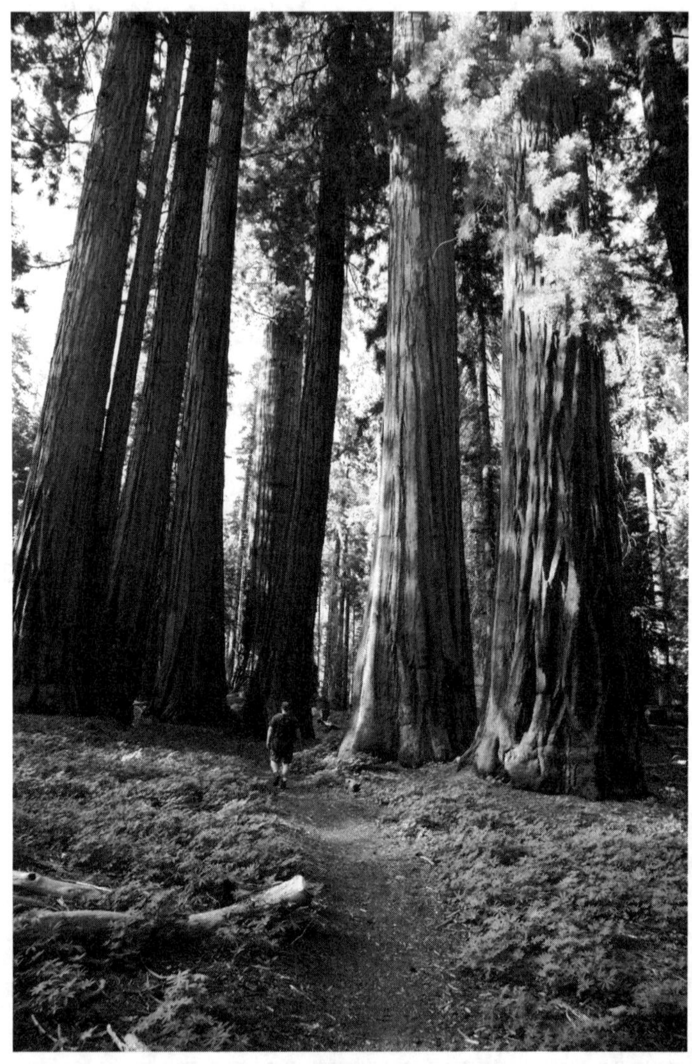

▲ Redwood forests need to be saved!

Saving redwood forests can help protect environments all over the Earth. The health of Earth's ecosystems depends on the perfect balance of carbon dioxide and oxygen in the atmosphere. Like all plants, redwoods take in carbon dioxide and give off oxygen. This helps keep Earth's atmosphere balanced.

Saving Giants (continued)

Why are redwoods in danger? Logging. Logging, cutting trees for timber, is the biggest threat. Logging damages habitats because it destroys natural homes for many animals. Owls, deer, chipmunks, and foxes are just a few animals that depend on the redwood forests. Salmon live in the streams that flow through these forests, and many endangered animals make their homes in the forests. If we care about animals, we must protect the animals' habitats.

While some people might think that we should stop logging all redwoods, there is a way to compromise. Let's face it. Logging companies need to stay in business, and redwood forests are a great source of timber. I believe loggers need to rethink which trees they cut down. They should choose smaller, weaker trees, and let the rest grow. This type of logging conserves natural resources. It uses fewer redwoods than were cut down in the past. This way we will not destroy all the redwoods and loggers can stay in business. If we use the redwood forests without wasting them, everyone and everything can benefit.

▲ Redwoods are the world's tallest trees.

How does the author use reasons to support his opinions?

____

____

How does the author use evidence to support his opinions?

____

____

Edit and Proofread

Choose the Editing and Proofreading Marks you need to correct the passage. Look for and correct the following:

- present-tense action verbs
- present progressive

Editing and Proofreading Marks

∧	Add.
℘	Take out.
⬭∧	Move to here.
∧,	Add comma.
⊙	Add period.

You probably don't realize just how much water you use at home. I is trying to figure it out. Let's see what I come up with.

When you brushes your teeth, you need water. After breakfast, you rinses your dishes. That's more water being used!

When we am washing the dog, we use a big bucket of soapy water. And don't forget about washing the car. My sister and I scrubs the headlights but that takes water, too.

This doesn't even count laundry and cooking! That soup are simmering on the stove with six quarts of water in it.

When you thinks about it, we have to be very watchful about the way we use water. Once it's down the drain, you can't get it back.

The Storm

Grammar Rules — Present and Present-Progressive Verbs

A **present-tense action verb** tells about an action that happens now or all the time. Add *-s* or *-es* to most action verbs to tell what one person, animal, or thing does.	The rain **pours** down. Ana **dashes** to the porch. Her dog **scurries** to her side.
A **present-progressive verb** tells about an action as it is happening. Use *am*, *is*, or *are* with a main verb that ends in *-ing*.	The water **is beating** on the roof. Giant puddles **are forming** in the yard. I **am staying** inside!

Circle the word or phrase that completes each sentence.

1. Dark clouds (gather/gathers) in the sky.

2. An icy wind (is whipping/are whipping) through the trees.

3. A storm (is approaching/are approaching) from the east.

4. The windows (is rattling/are rattling) from the wind.

5. The storm (pass/passes) the small town.

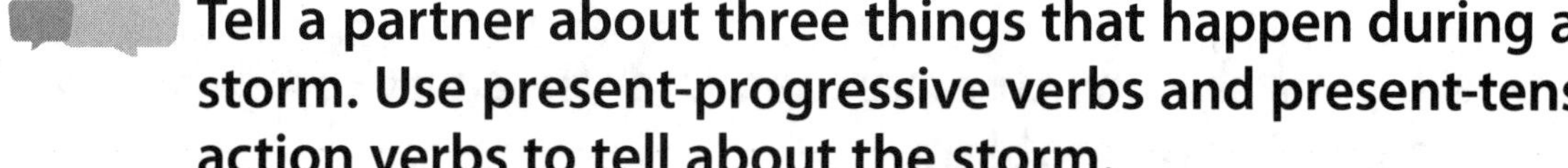

Tell a partner about three things that happen during a storm. Use present-progressive verbs and present-tense action verbs to tell about the storm.

Problem and Solution

Make a problem-and-solution chart to tell about a problem that you solved.

Problem-and-Solution Chart

Problem:

Event 1:

Event 2:

Solution:

 **Share your chart with a partner. Use the chart to tell how you solved your problem.**

PM4.17

Helping the Environment

recycle	conserve	trickle
evaporate	float	predict

1. Choose an action verb from the chart.

2. Challenge your partner to use it in a sentence about the environment. The sentence must also use a form of the helping verb *do* or *have*. The form of the action verb may have to change to make the sentence correct.

3. If the sentence is correct, your partner gets one point. If the sentence is not correct, you get one point.

4. Then your partner chooses a word and you must make a sentence.

5. Continue playing until you each have used all the words.

Edit and Proofread

Choose the Editing and Proofreading Marks you need to correct the passage. Look for:

- correct linking verbs
- correct helping verbs

Editing and Proofreading Marks

∧	Add.
℘	Take out.
⌒∧	Move to here.
∧	Add comma.
⊙	Add period.

My cousins am farmers. A few years ago, Cousin Marc became

concerned, "I do not think I cans add any more chemicals to this

land," he said one night. "Can we make our farm organic?"

Cousin James felt unsure. "It seem hard to imagine farming

without chemicals," he said. "Organic farming must work.

Others has accomplished it."

That was five years ago. I are visiting the farm this week, and it

are thriving! Cousin Marc musts spray some of the vegetables with

pepper oil to keep away certain pests. Cousin James are planting

basil plants to help repel pests from the tomatoes.

I is astonished at how much their farm yields.

Test-Taking Strategy Practice

Understand the Question

Directions: Read each question about "Doña Flor." Choose the best answer.

Sample

> **❶** How did the people in the village use the extra tortillas that Doña Flor made?
>
> Ⓐ They ate the tortillas for breakfast.
>
> ● They used the tortillas as roofs and rafts.
>
> Ⓒ They used the tortillas as an alarm clock.
>
> Ⓓ They were the best tortillas in the world.

❷ What caused the village people to hide in their homes?

Ⓐ The river was flowing.

Ⓑ It was raining.

Ⓒ They were waiting for tortillas.

Ⓓ They heard a mountain lion.

❸ What did the puma use to make his roars louder to scare the villagers?

Ⓐ the canyon

Ⓑ a hollow log

Ⓒ a deep breath

Ⓓ Doña Flor

 **How did you use the test-taking strategy to answer the question?**

For use with TE p. T268   **PM4.20**   **Unit 4 | Power of Nature**

Problem-and-Solution Chart

"Doña Flor"

Complete a problem-and-solution chart to retell the story of "Doña Flor."

Problem: Puma frightens Doña Flor's friends.

Event 1:
Event 2:
Event 3:

Solution:

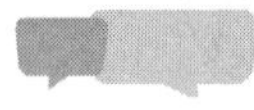

Use your problem-and-solution chart to retell the story for a partner.

Unit 4 | Power of Nature

"Doña Flor"

Use this passage to practice reading with proper expression.

Doña Flor just smiled at that brave cat and said, "Why, you're 12

just a kitten to me, Pumito." She bent down and scratched that 24

puma behind the ears, and she whispered to him in cat talk 36

until that cat began to purr. 42

Suddenly Flor heard a new noise. "Doña Flor, ¿dónde estás? 52

Where are you?" called her worried neighbors. Even though they 62

were frightened, they had all come, holding hands, looking for her. 73

"Meet my new amigo," said Doña Flor. 80

That evening, Flor plucked a star and plunked it on the tallest 92

tree so her friends in the pueblo could find their way home. 104

From "Doña Flor," page 264

Expression

1 ☐ Does not read with feeling.

2 ☐ Reads with some feeling, but does not match content.

3 ☐ Reads with appropriate feeling for most content.

4 ☐ Reads with appropriate feeling for all content.

Accuracy and Rate Formula

Use the formula to measure a reader's accuracy and rate while reading aloud.

_________ − _________ = _________

words attempted in one minute | number of errors | words correct per minute (wcpm)

The Library

Grammar Rules Linking and Helping Verbs

Linking verbs like *be*, *seem*, *become*, and *feel* connect the subject to a part of the predicate that tells about the subject.	Mara **is** a wonderful storyteller. Her characters **seem** so real. Mara **feels** proud of her stories.
Some verbs are made up of more than one word. A **helping verb** like *do*, *does*, *can*, *may*, *might*, and *must* comes before the **main verb**.	We <u>**do**</u> enjoy trips to the library. The librarian <u>**can**</u> find several books for us. I <u>**may**</u> request his help again. He <u>**might**</u> have more books.

**Read the sentences below. Underline linking verbs.
Circle helping verbs.**

1. Mrs. Kim is a marine biologist at the aquarium.

2. Our teachers can invite her to our classes.

3. Mrs. Kim seems friendly and helpful.

4. She may tell us about her work with sea animals.

5. We can ask her questions about her work.

 **With a partner, role-play a conversation between Mrs. Kim and a student. Take turns asking and answering questions that use linking and helping verbs.**

Answer the Question

Read a question to your partner. Have your partner change the question to an answer and write the new sentence. Remember to use the helping verb.

1. Should we supply water for the hike?

____

2. Could Keiko alter the route that we follow?

____

3. Would you and Arnie guide us if we ask you to?

____

____

4. Could coyotes stray into the campground?

____

5. Would I feel safer on higher ground?

____

After all the answers are written, take turns using the helping verbs *could, should,* and *would* to ask and answer six more questions about things in the environment. Here is an example: *Could it rain today? Yes, it could rain today.* Partners get one point for each answer that correctly uses *could, should* or *would*.

Speed Sentences

1. **Cut apart the cards. Place the gray main verb cards face up in a pile. Spread out the white helping verb cards and place them face down.**

2. **Together, count "One, two, three!" Players quickly take one white card and read it aloud. The first person to read the word aloud draws a gray card and says a sentence using the helping verb on the white card and the main verb on the gray card. The player keeps the white card and returns the gray card.**

3. **Play until everyone has had a chance to make at least two sentences.**

do	did	have	plant
has	can	might	harvest
must	should	would	irrigate
does	may	could	cultivate

Compare Figurative Language

Write examples of figurative language from the story and poems.
Explain what they mean.

Title	Example/Type	What It Means	What You Picture
"Doña Flor"	"the houses smelled corn good" metaphor	The houses smelled like corn, which smells good.	I picture a kitchen with people eating.
"Comida"			
"The Sun in Me"			

Compare charts with a partner. Discuss the examples of figurative language you found. Compare what they mean.

Grammar: Practice

The Moon Is...

Grammar Rules Forms of *be* and *have*

The verbs *be* and *have* must agree with the subject.

	be	have
• Use for *I*:	am	have
• Use for *you, we,* or *they* and plural subjects:	are	have
• Use for *he, she,* or *it* and singular subjects:	is	has

Complete the sentences with forms of the verbs *to be* or *to have*. Use contractions if a subject is missing.

"The moon ___*is*___ Swiss Cheese," I said. "_________ serious! It

_________ holes all over it."

"_________ silly," said my sister. "The holes _________ craters.

They look like holes but _________ not. We _________ a book about

the moon. _________ in the house."

"Well, get it quickly. Hungry mice _________ on the moon," I said.

"Look, _________ eaten almost all of it."

 **Read your latest writing activity to a partner. Tell how you used forms of *be* and *have*. Fix any that may be incorrect.**

Myth Talk
BY CASSANDRA TROY

The Breakfast Goddess

Ceres was a goddess you would like to meet.
She was mother to crops on the farm.
Nurturing grains such as barley and wheat,
She protected and kept them from harm.

We still remember Ceres's tender care
When each morning we gather to eat
The bowls of cereal that her name still bear.
Hail! Goddess of our breakfast treat!

> How does the name Ceres help you
> understand the meaning of *cereal*?

▲ Ceres

Echo's Echo

Echo's sweet voice her own words spoke clear
Till goddess Hera, in anger, cried, "Hold!"
When Echo's next words winged around our sphere,
They just repeated what others had told.

When your voice interacts with a big empty place,
Does the echo you hear sound quite near?
Just shout a "Hello!" into all of that space,
And what do you think you will hear?

> How does the name Echo help you understand
> the meaning of *echo*?

▲ Echo

Mark-Up Reading

Myth Talk (continued)

Pan, the Troublemaker

The Greek god of nature in the wild,
Pan caused trouble any way he could.
His eerie screams clutched man or child,
So they ran madly through the wood.

The outcome of Pan's type of game
Reminds us of him today.
When we say people panic, we use
Pan's name,
To show that folks act in what way?

▲ Pan

> How does the name Pan help you
> understand the meaning of *panic*?

Reflecting on Narcissus

Narcissus was a handsome lad.
Greek women hoped to win his heart.
Instead he made them very sad
And, cold as ice, stood apart.

Narcissus, looking into a pool,
Fell in love with what he'd seen.
Now if we call a silly fool
A narcissist, what do we mean?

▲ Narcissus

> How does the name Narcissus help you
> understand the meaning of *narcissist*?

Edit and Proofread

Choose the Editing and Proofreading Marks you need to correct the passage. Look for the following:

- correct helping verbs
- correct forms of *be* and *have*
- correct contractions

Editing and Proofreading Marks

∧	Add.
⌇	Take out.
⌒∧	Move to here.
∧,	Add comma.
⊙	Add period.

What would you like better, hiking along mountain trails or tubing down a river? I're sure that I would like tubing better, but my dad and I am debating the topic.

Dad said, "The sun cans burn you when you are on the water." He do not realize that the sun is pretty hot on the mountain.

I said that could we fall on the rocky mountain trails. He replied, "Yes, but those tubes could flip over. We better has lifejackets on."

After a while, we stopped our debate. Dad said, "We shoulds try them both. It is the only way to know." He am excited about this adventure in nature. I have a feeling that we's going to like both.

The Big Event

Grammar Rules Helping Verbs

Helping verbs work with **main verbs**. The main verbs tell what the subject does.	We **are** cheering for the team. The player **is struggling** to win.
The **helping verbs** *be*, *have*, and *do* change to match the subject.	The goalie **does block** the ball. The players **do run** very quickly.
The **helping verbs** *can*, *may*, *might*, *must*, *should*, *would*, and *could* do not change.	We **can go** to the game on Friday. Ethan **can play**. The other children **can play**, too.

Use the correct form of the helping verb to complete each sentence. Then read the sentences to a partner.

1. Ana's family __________ camping by the Grand Canyon this summer.
   (be)

2. Her mom __________ planned all the details.
   (have)

3. The kids __________ pack their own bags.
   (should)

4. Ana's father __________ bring the tents.
   (can)

5. Both of her parents __________ be ready to explore nature!
   (must)

Imagine you are getting ready for a big event like a vacation or an important game. Tell a partner what you are planning to do.

Invaders!

**Make a concept map with the answers to the Big Question:
When do harmless things become harmful?**

A Fast-Growing Plant

Complete the events chain for your partner's story about a fast-growing plant.

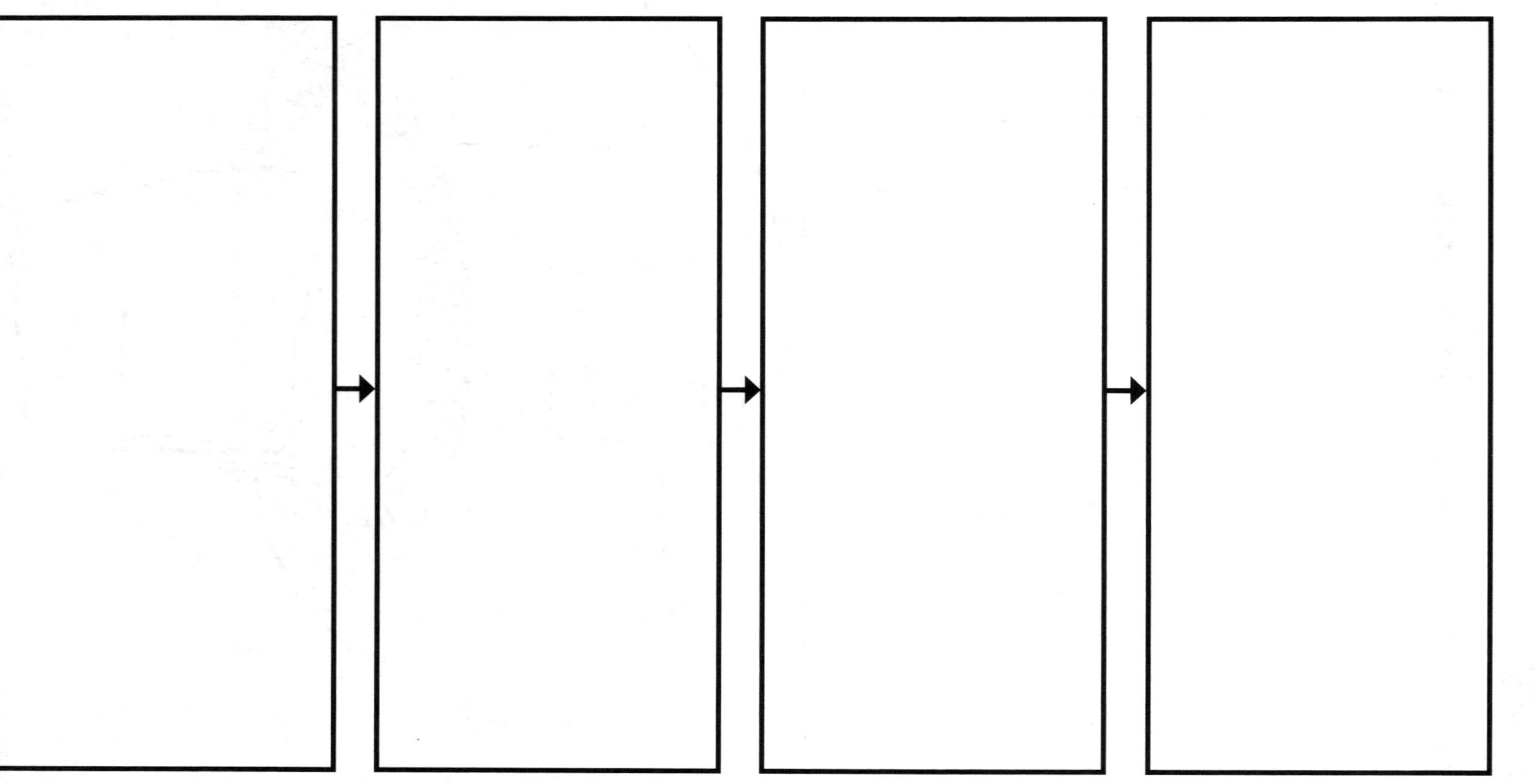

Use your events chain to retell your partner's story.

Grammar: Game

Spin a Contraction

1. Take turns spinning the spinner.
2. Read aloud the sentence that you land on. Then repeat the sentence, replacing the underlined words with a contraction. Say and spell the contraction.
3. Play until you have changed all the sentences.

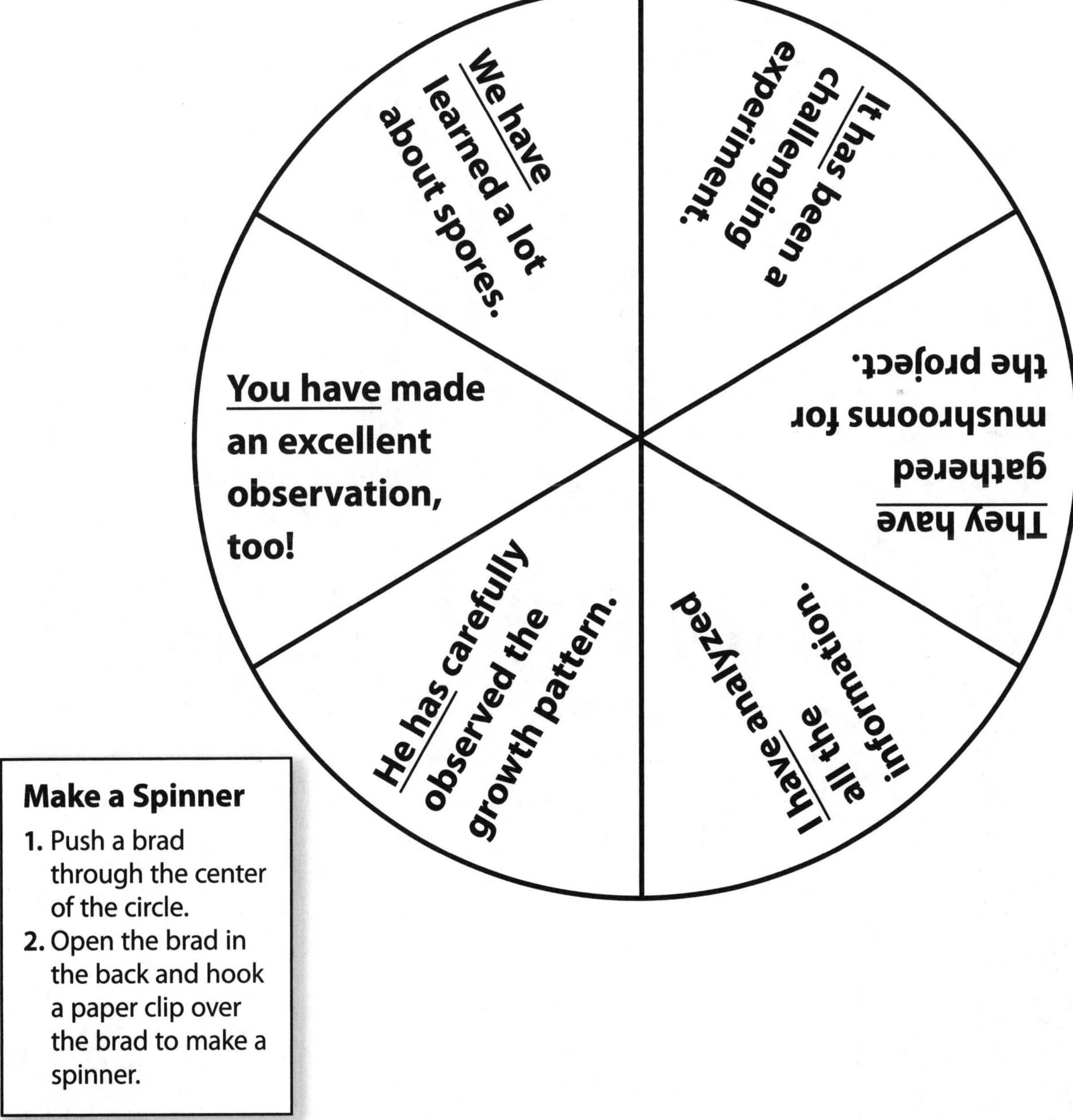

Make a Spinner

1. Push a brad through the center of the circle.
2. Open the brad in the back and hook a paper clip over the brad to make a spinner.

Edit and Proofread

Choose the Editing and Proofreading Marks you need to correct the passage. Look for contractions with the following words:

- *am, are, is*
- *have, has*
- *not*

Editing and Proofreading Marks

∧	Add.
℘	Take out.
⌄	Add apostrophe.
⋏	Add comma.
⊙	Add period.

"Im ready to start the experiment if you are," Josh said.

"Just a minute," I answered. "We have'nt got a glass."

"Yes, we do," Josh said. "Its on the floor."

I picked up the glass, and Josh poured vinegar in it. Then I dropped a rock in the vinegar.

"Im'm not sure what wer'e looking for," I muttered. "What is the vinegar supposed to do?"

"Were looking for bubbles in the vinegar—and there they are!" Josh cried. "We'ave just proved that this rock is limestone."

"We have?" I said.

Unit 5 | Invaders!

Know the Test Format

Directions: Read the questions about "The Fungus that Ate My School." Choose the best answer.

Sample

1 When the students returned from spring vacation, the school was covered with fungus. In which month did the students mmost likely return to school?

Ⓐ December

Ⓑ August

● April

Ⓓ November

2 The fungus ate Alex's __________ .

Ⓐ lunch

Ⓑ notebook

Ⓒ homework

Ⓓ pencil

3 Who thinks that the fungus is a treasure?

Ⓐ Professor Macademia

Ⓑ Mr. Page

Ⓒ Mr. Harrison

Ⓓ Ellen

 **Tell a partner how you used the strategy to answer the questions.**

PM5.5

Events Chain

"The Fungus That Ate My School"

Make an events chain to tell what happens in "The Fungus That Ate My School."

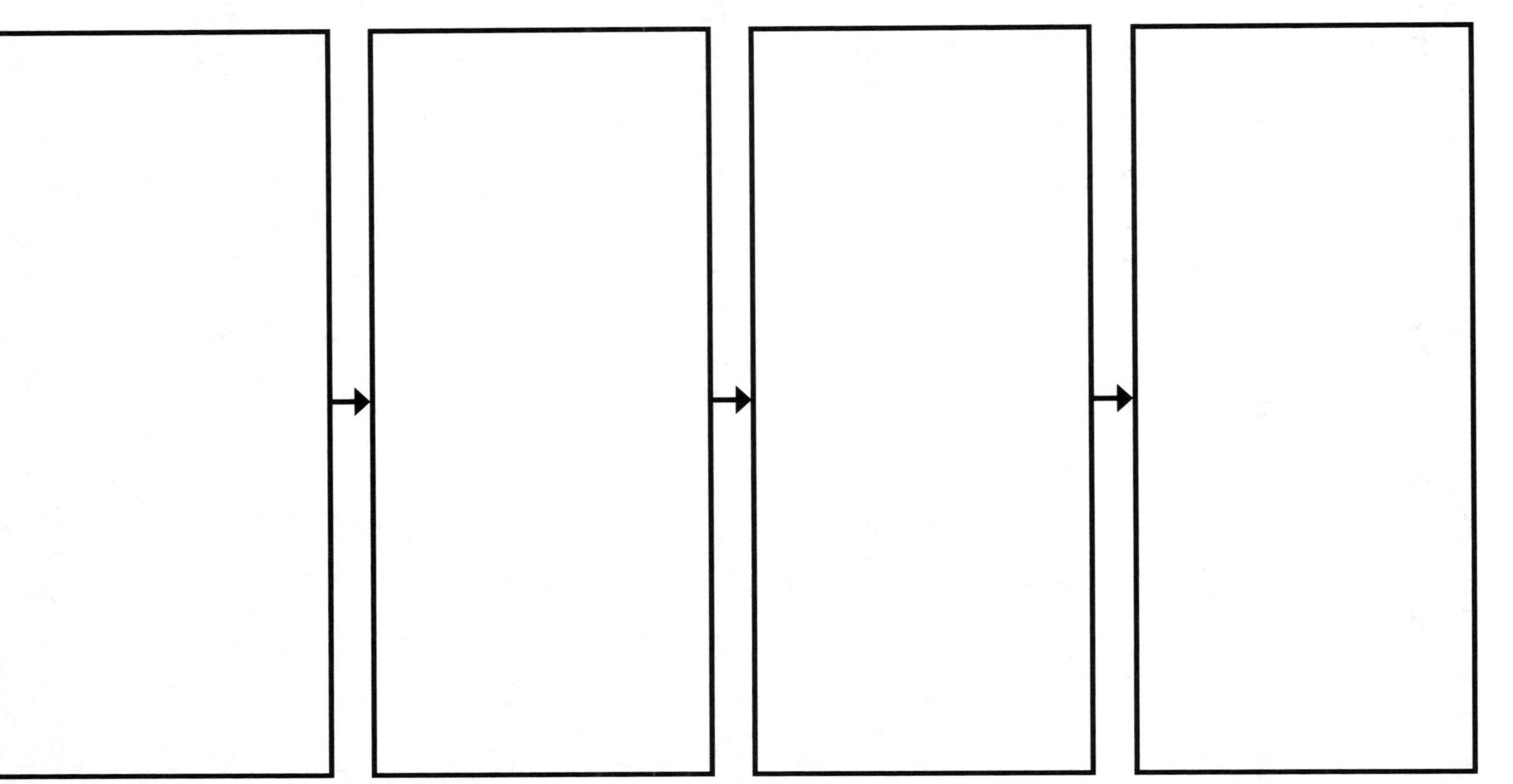

Share your events chain to retell the story to a partner.

"The Fungus That Ate My School"

**Expression is how you use your voice to express feeling.
Use this passage to practice reading with proper expression.**

"Fresh air, light, elbow grease, and a little help from my friends in the   14

Fungus Unit ought to get rid of IT," said Professor Macademia.   25

"Fungus Unit? What's a Fungus Unit?" Ellen asked.   33

"Special branch of the Sanitation Department," said someone dressed in   43

white, pulling a giant hose into the school. Other workers carried in shovels,   56

mops, and big lights.   60

"Action!" called one of them.   65

Suddenly the whole school was filled with whirring and clanking,   75

swooshing and scrubbing.   78

From "The Fungus that Ate My School," page 298

Expression

1 ☐ Does not read with feeling.   3 ☐ Reads with appropriate feeling for most content.

2 ☐ Reads with some feeling, but does not match content.   4 ☐ Reads with appropriate feeling for all content.

Accuracy and Rate Formula
Use the formula to measure a reader's accuracy and rate while reading aloud.

__________ −	__________ =	__________
words attempted in one minute	number of errors	words correct per minute (wcpm)

Name ____ Date _______________________

What's for Lunch?

Grammar Rules: Contractions

A **contraction** is two words put together. It leaves out a letter or letters. A contraction can be made from • a subject and a verb • a verb and the word *not*. An **apostrophe** shows where the letter or letters have been left out.	I am hungry. I'm hungry. Jacob does not like his lunch. Jacob doesn't like his lunch.
The subject and verb agree. The verb and *not* agree.	They are not having lunch. They aren't having lunch.

Circle the correct contraction that completes each sentence.

1. Madison (Madisons/Madison's) in the cafeteria today.
2. Every day, (you've/youve) liked what (shes/she's) made.
3. They (doesn't/don't) know how good her food is.
4. Jacob (haven't/hasn't) even tried her lunches.
5. It (isn't/aren't) an expensive lunch. (Its/It's) a good deal.

 **Tell a partner about what you and your friends like and don't like for lunch. Use contractions to tell about lunch.**

Cumulative Story

In a group of four students, write each word in the box on a separate index card. Sit in a circle and place four cards face down in the middle. Set the other four aside.

round	**huge**	**sharp**	**long**
squishy	**bumpy**	**fuzzy**	**slimy**

Build a story with the word cards and this story starter:

In the science lab, I saw _____________ .

1. Choose one student to start. Student 1 draws a card and completes the story starter, using the adjective on his or her card to describe a noun of their choice.
   For example: *In the science lab I saw a **slimy** octopus.*
2. The student to the right of Student 1 draws a card, repeats the first sentence, and then adds a second sentence to the story, using his or her adjective before a noun.
3. Continue until everyone in the circle has repeated the previous sentences and added a new one according to the rules.
4. Try to remember the whole story and say it together!
5. Play another round with the last four adjective cards.

Predicate Adjective Hunt

Some of these sentences contain a predicate adjective. Underline each predicate adjective. Circle the linking verb. Then draw an arrow from the predicate adjective to the noun or pronoun it describes.

1. An American scientist conducted the research.

2. After the experiment, the egg was rotten.

3. This article about the moon looks interesting.

4. He drew a simple diagram of the plant.

5. It seems impossible to me.

6. I measured the exact amount of rainfall.

7. The chemistry students studied for a test.

8. Her observations were accurate.

Bonus Sentence: I am ___________________________ !

Compare Author's Purpose

Put a check mark by each purpose that fits the science fiction story or the science experiment.

Purpose of Genre	Science Fiction Story	Science Experiment
Tells about a science idea	✓	
Tests a science idea		✓
Tells how to do something		
Is mostly fun to read		
Describes events that can't really happen		

 **Discuss each author's purpose with a partner. Together, write sentences to tell why an author writes a science fiction story and why an author writes a science experiment.**

Gross or Good?

Plural Nouns **Adjectives**

1. Use adjectives to tell about color, size, or shape: **pink, brown, small, long**

2. Use adjectives to tell how something sounds, feels, looks, tastes, or smells: **loud**, **wet**, **slimy**, **salty**, **smoky**

3. Use adjectives to tell how something is used: **fishing pole**, **frying pan**, **sleeping bag**

4. Use adjectives to compare two things: **damper, brighter**

5. Use adjectives to compare more than two things: **biggest**, **wettest**

Choose an adjective from the box above to complete each sentence. Write the adjective on the line.

At night, Dad and I are crowded in our ___*small*___ tent. We hear

the __________ rain outside. In the morning, the sun is __________

than the day before. But the ground is __________ than before. Gross!

We have been invaded by __________ worms! Dad takes out his

__________ pole. "These __________ worms are the __________ gift,"

says Dad. Now we can catch the __________ fish of all!

Talk with a partner about a gross plant or animal you've seen. Use adjectives to describe and make comparisons.

Don't Be Terrorized by
Termites!

Did you know that tiny bugs called termites can eat whole houses? Don't let that happen to you! ACT NOW to control the spread of these invaders! Unprotected homes may lead to homeowners spending a lot of money to fix termite damage. Americans spend about $1 billion a year repairing damage caused by termites. Join other smart homeowners!

Try our pest prevention service today!

▲ There are 2,750 known species of termites.

Home Protection Tips

If you see termites on your walk through a forest, have no fear. Termites are fine if you keep them outside your house. It's inside your house that requires immediate action.

First, make sure no wood in your home touches wet soil. Termites can survive in dry wood, but damp wood invites termites to enter!

Next, seal any cracks you find around the outside of your home, no matter how tiny! Some cracks may seem small, but they are still big enough for termites to enter. Remember, termites are only about half an inch long.

Finally, keep firewood away from your home and off the ground. Firewood is a feast for termites! They will start by eating the firewood, but may not stop until they've chewed through the pine paneling in your dining room.

Don't Be Terrorized by Termites! (continued)

What if termites have already moved in?

How can you know if termites are already inside your home? Small holes in your woodwork or sawdust-like termite droppings are evidence of a termite infestation. Our experts are the best in the business. They have been thoroughly trained to spot all signs of termites. Don't delay! Do what your smartest neighbors are doing. Schedule a home inspection today!

There are several treatments for a termite infestation. For small infestations, we might treat the wood with extreme heat or extreme cold to kill the termites. Then we can create a termite-proof barrier by treating the soil around the house with insecticide to prevent these pests from ever getting back in.

▲ Trained experts know how to spot termite damage.

Let us assist you in keeping your home termite-free! With our help, you can keep termites from getting in or get rid of termites and keep them from coming back. Now that is money well spent! Call to schedule a home visit today.

Explain how the reasons, evidence, and persuasive techniques help the author achieve the purpose of the ad.

____

____

____

Grammar: Grammar and Writing

Edit and Proofread

Choose the Editing and Proofreading Marks you need to correct the passage. Look for the following:

- correct placement of adjectives, making sure to have at least two predicate adjectives
- correct formation of adjectives that compare

Editing and Proofreading Marks

∧	Add.
ℒ	Take out.
⊂⊃∧	Move to here.
∧̦	Add comma.
⊙	Add period.

My friends and I love movies silly about scientists who try to stop monsters big that attack cities. Last night we watched an old movie like that on TV. It great was. A creature slimy crawled out of a river and terrorized New York. The creature was tallest than the Empire State Building. The president ordered the smarter scientist in the country to stop it. Other scientists brilliant volunteered to help.

It took the scientists a time long to figure out what to do. In the meantime, the city was a mess! The creature huge stepped on cars and knocked over skyscrapers. The people hysterical were!

Finally, the scientists realized that a plant that grew on the taller mountain in North America could destroy the beast. A hero got the plant, and the scientists used it to kill the creature!

My Old House

Grammar Rules: Adjectives

An **adjective** describes, or tells about, a noun or a pronoun. Use adjectives to tell how something sounds, feels, looks, tastes, or smells.	The creaky stairs in my old home make loud noises.
An adjective that follows a <u>linking verb</u> is a **predicate adjective**. It describes a noun or pronoun in the subject.	My home <u>is</u> old. The stairs <u>are</u> creaky.

Underline the adjectives in each sentence.

1. My red home was a pretty place, but a small home.
2. I liked the fresh garden in our big yard.
3. My new home is big, but it needs nice paint.
4. The home looks good with blue paint.
5. My happy family likes the new paint.

 **Tell a partner about where you live. Use adjectives and predicate adjectives to describe your place**

Name _______________________________ Date _______________

Identify Problem and Solution

Make a problem-and-solution chart about a problem in your environment.

Problem-and-Solution Chart

Problem:

Example:

Example:

Example:

Solution:

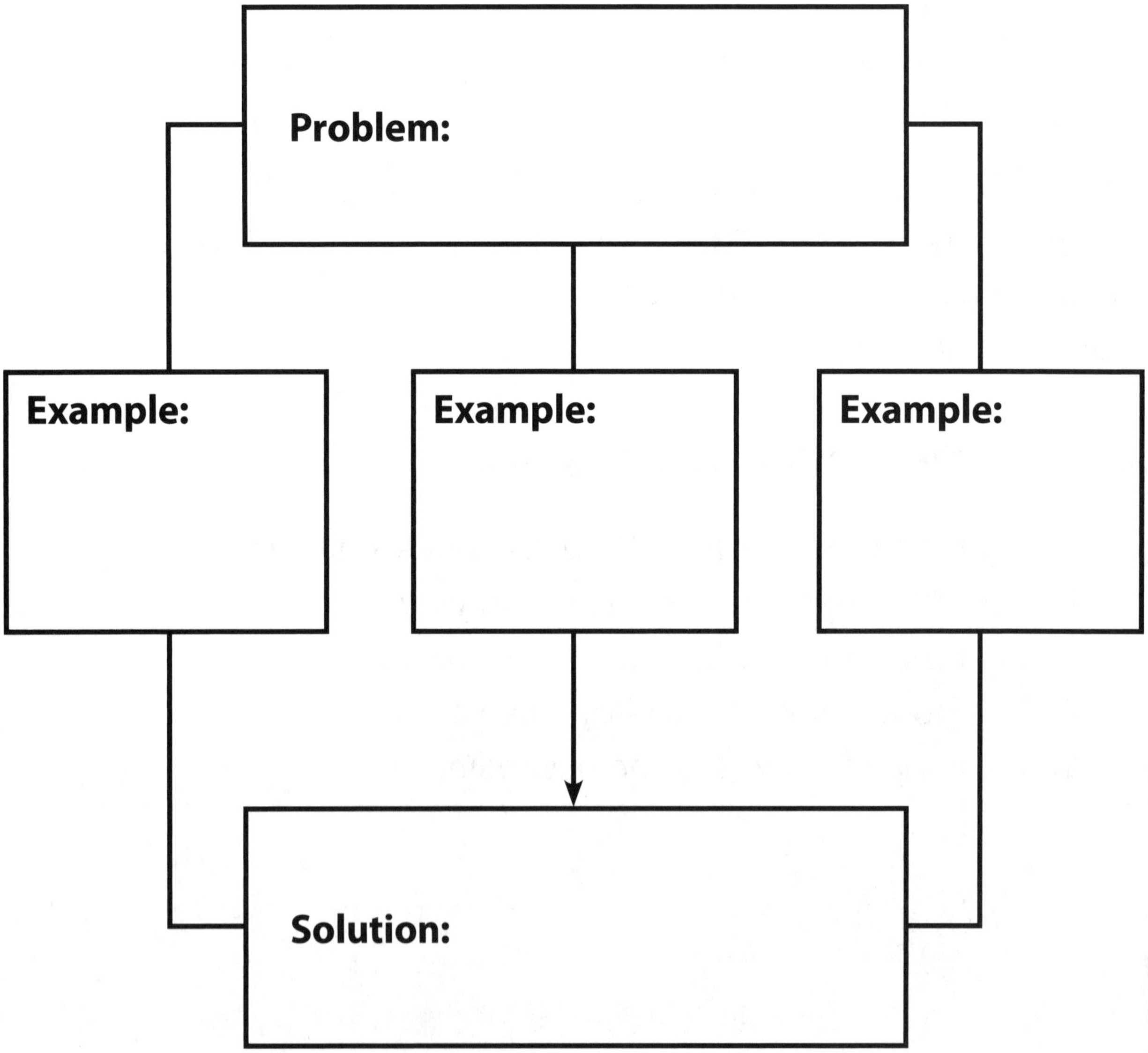

 **Share your chart with another pair of partners and see if you can come up with more solutions.**

Word Race

thick	dangerous	green	important	delicate
serious	happy	interesting	large	healthy

1. Write a different adjective from the box on each game board space.

2. Flip a coin. Move one space for heads. Move two spaces for tails.

3. Read the adjective aloud. Use it in a sentence that compares two things. Use this sentence frame: This/These ___________ is/are ___________ than ___________.

4. The first player to reach the finish wins.

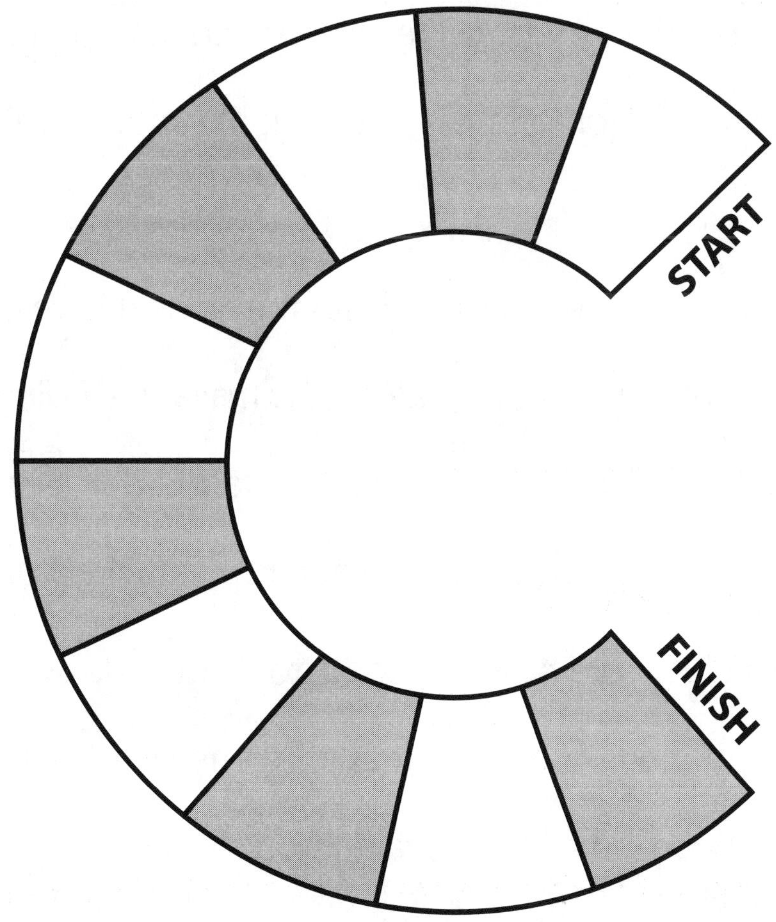

Edit and Proofread

Choose the Editing and Proofreading Marks you need to correct the passage. Look for correct usage of these comparison adjectives:

- *-er than* and *more . . . than*
- *the -est* and *the most*
- irregular forms

Editing and Proofreading Marks

∧	Add.
✐	Take out.
⌒∧	Move to here.
∧,	Add comma.
⊙	Add period.

The lake near our home has ~~fewer~~ less water this year than it had last year. This has been the worse year on record for rainfall in a decade, so the lake has really shrunk. Sometimes I think it looks more small than a backyard pool!

Yet only a few years ago, the water level was the higher I have ever seen. You could see all kinds of birds on the water. I saw mallard ducklings that were the cuter than stuffed toys. The most amazingest bird of all, though, was the snowy egret. I think it is the more beautiful bird in the world.

The plants around the lake have changed, too. They look withered than they did last summer—brownest than dirt! The lake used to be the prettier than it is now, so we hope the rain returns. That would be the better thing of all that could happen!

Reread

**Read each question about "Aliens from Earth."
Choose the best answer.**

Sample

---

1 Why does kudzu grow more quickly in the southeastern states than in Japan?

Ⓐ Kudzu grows better in forests.

Ⓑ There is more sunlight in the southeastern states.

● The warm, humid climate makes the plant grow quickly.

Ⓓ Kudzu has more room to grow in the southeastern states.

---

2 Why did the rabbit population explode in Australia?

Ⓐ There was a law that no one could kill rabbits.

Ⓑ They had no natural predators.

Ⓒ The Europeans brought over too many rabbits.

Ⓓ They had plenty of food.

3 How did zebra mussels invade the United States?

Ⓐ They came from Europe on buoys.

Ⓑ They came from Europe in ballast tanks.

Ⓒ Birds brought them over.

Ⓓ Scientists thought they would help local fishermen.

Tell a partner how you used the strategy to answer the questions.

Name _________________________________ Date _________________

"Aliens from Earth"

Complete a problem-and-solution chart to tell about the main problem in "Aliens from Earth."

Problem-and-Solution Chart

Problem:
Alien species threaten native species and harm their habitat.

Example 1:

Example 2:

Example 3:

Solution:

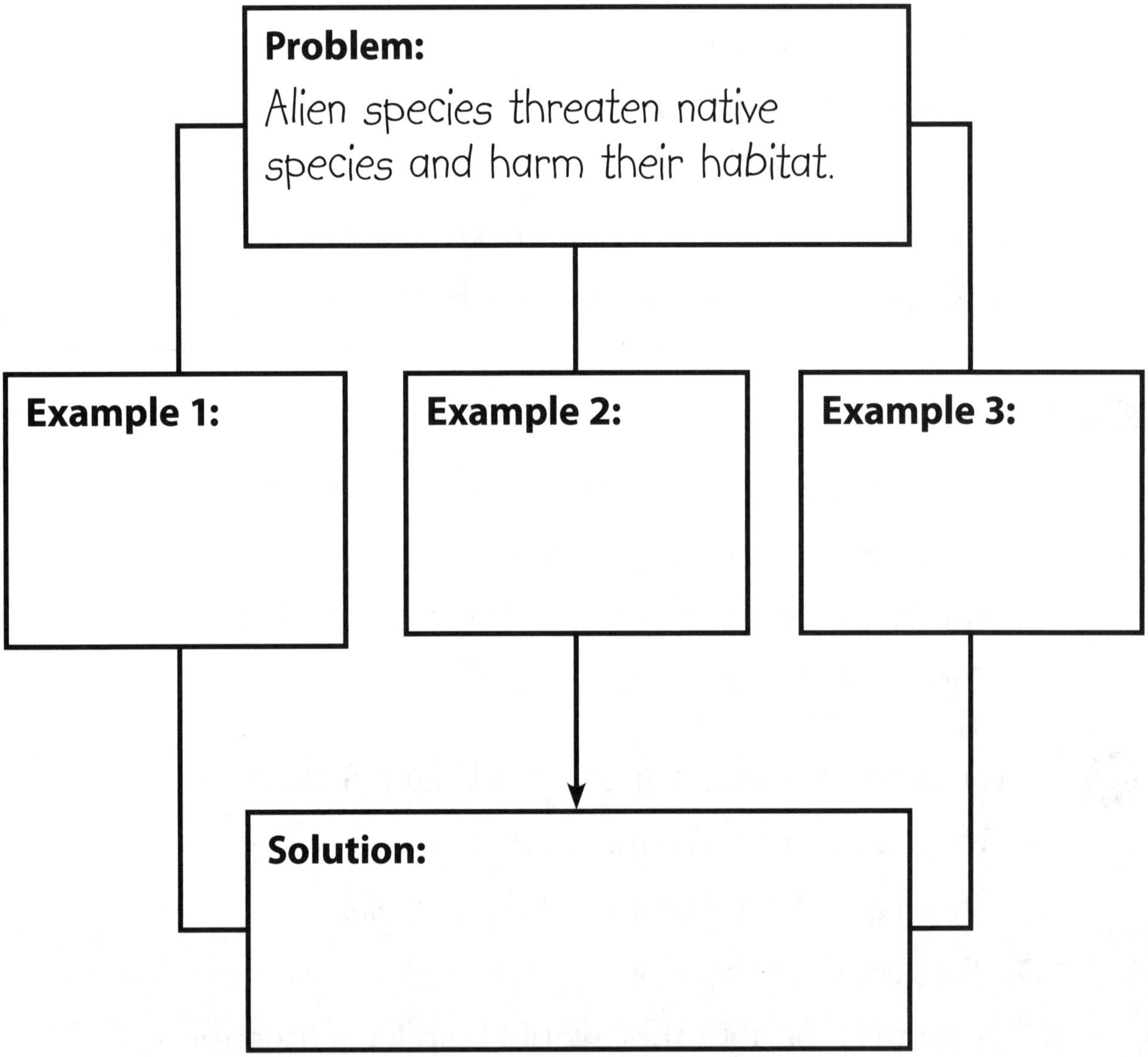

 **Use your problem-and-solution chart to summarize the text for a partner.**

Fluency Practice

"Aliens from Earth"

Use this passage to practice reading with proper phrasing.

Phrasing is how you use your voice to group words together. Punctuation marks such as periods and commas can help you group words into phrases. Use this passage to practice reading with appropriate phrasing.

Many aliens arrive in the ballast tanks of cargo ships.   10

Filled with seawater, these large tanks help ships stay   19

balanced. The tanks are like aquariums in the middle   28

of the ship. When a ship arrives in port, it empties   39

its ballast tank. This action releases thousands of   47

worms, clams, snails, and other sea creatures into an   56

ecosystem where they do not belong.   62

From "Aliens from Earth," page 330

Phrasing

| 1 | ☐ Rarely pauses while reading the text. | 3 | ☐ Frequently pauses at appropriate points in the text. |
| 2 | ☐ Occasionally pauses while reading the text. | 4 | ☐ Consistently pauses at all appropriate points in the text. |

Accuracy and Rate Formula
Use the formula to measure a reader's accuracy and rate while reading aloud.

____________ − ____________ = ____________
words attempted   number of errors   words correct per minute
in one minute   (wcpm)

The Race of the Pets

Grammar Rules: Adjectives

Use **comparison adjectives** to compare <u>two</u> <u>things</u> • Add *-er* to most adjectives followed by *than*. • Add *more,* followed by *than* when the adjective has three or more syllables.	Sonya has two cats. Sparky is bigg<u>er</u> <u>than</u> Paws. But I think that Paws is <u>more</u> beautiful <u>than</u> Sparky.
Use **comparison adjectives** to compare <u>three</u> <u>or</u> <u>more</u> <u>things</u> • Add *-est* to most adjectives, with *the* in front. • Add *most,* with *the* in front when the adjective has three or more syllables.	Sonya's puppy is the cut<u>est</u> of her pets. He is the <u>most</u> <u>energetic</u> pet.

Circle the word that correctly completes each sentence.

1. We put all six pets in a race to see who is the (fast/fastest)
2. Sparky was (slower/more slow) than Paws.
3. But Paws was (more interesting/interestinger) than Sparky.
4. Paws ran in circles. He was the (more/most) entertaining pet.
5. My pet won the race. She was the (more smart/smartest).

 **Tell a partner about a race you've seen. Use comparison adjectives to tell about the race.**

Grammar: Game

Adjectives in Order?

Directions:

1. Take turns choosing 2 of the 3 adjectives in a square and writing a sentence with the adjectives in the correct order. (They are not in the right order in the squares!) Put an X through the square to show that you have used it.

2. With your partner, use the **Order of Adjectives** box below to check the order of the adjectives in the sentence. If they are in the correct order, you get 1 point.

3. You will have 10 minutes to play. The winner is the player with more points when the timer rings.

Order of Adjectives

opinion → size → age → shape → color → origin → material → purpose

old, funny, gray	rectangular, long, blue	African, iron, unusual	sleeping, big, new
wavy, odd, wooden	green, Italian, interesting	garden, straw, huge	beautiful, yellow, round
walking, best, white	ancient, triangular, small	colorful, cotton, Mexican	gigantic, wonderful, silver

Grammar: Game

Make It Possessive!

Directions:

1. Cut out the cards and spread them out face up. Take turns selecting a white card and matching it with a gray card.

2. Spell the possessive noun: for example, *i-s-l-a-n-d-s apostrophe.*

3. If the other group members agree with your spelling, make up a phrase with the possessive noun (such as *the islands' trees*) and keep the white card.

4. If they don't agree, return your white card face up to the center. Move to the next player. Keep playing until all the white cards are gone.

's	'	islands	bird
plant	population	organisms	men
ants	flower	bees	rock
octopus	trees	mice	forest
children	roots	animals	atlas

For use with TE p. 337k   **PM5.25**   Unit 5 | Invaders!

Venn Diagram

Compare Genres

With a partner, compare and contrast the science text and science journal.
Then complete the Venn diagram for the two genres.

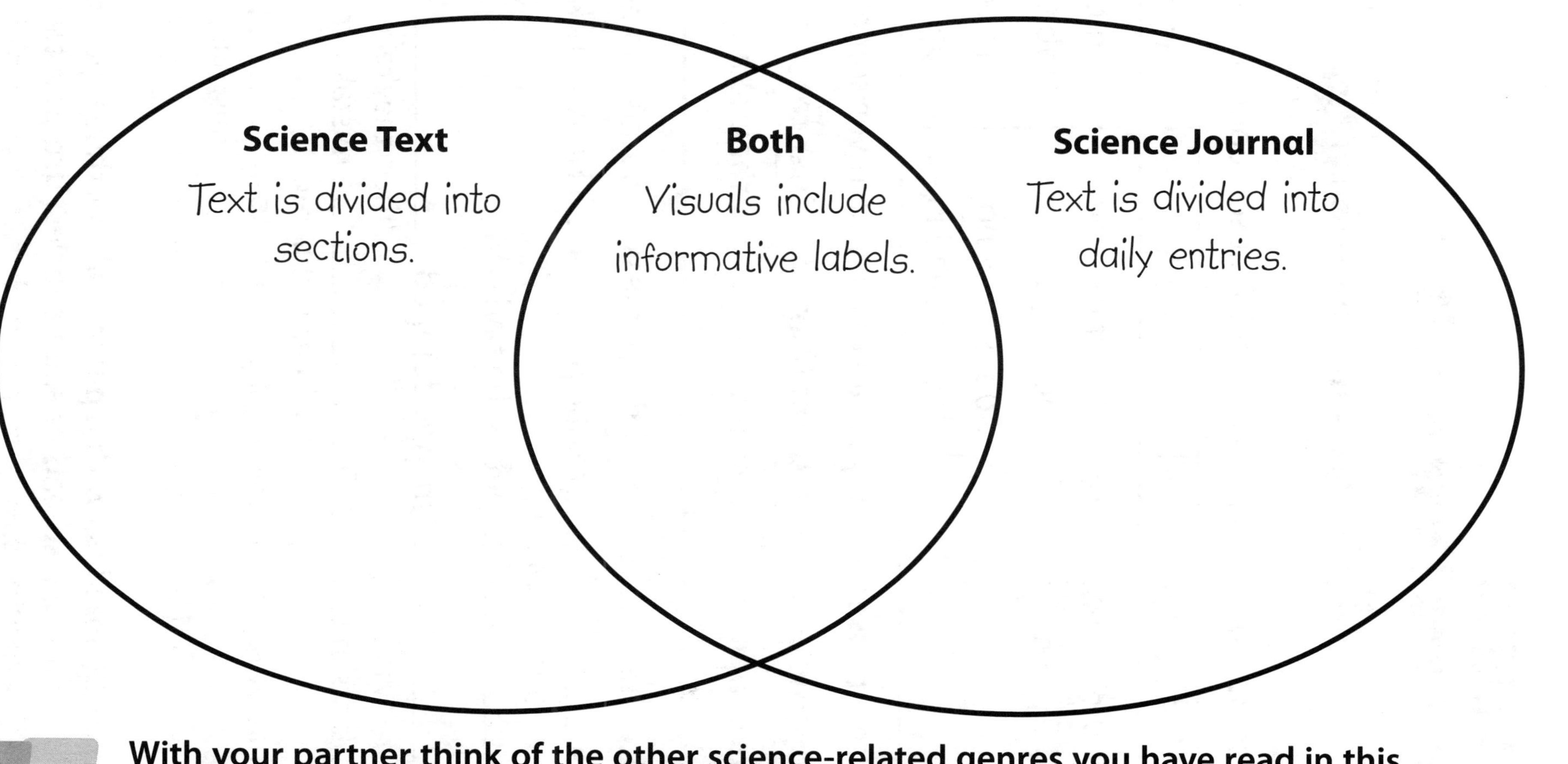

With your partner think of the other science-related genres you have read in this unit. Discuss what they have in common with the two genres compared above.

Protect Your Habitat

Grammar Rules Possessive Nouns and Adjectives

Use **possessive nouns** to show that someone owns something.

One Owner	Add **'s**	a **rabbit's** hole
More Than One Owner	Add **'** if the noun ends in **-s**. Add **'s** if the noun does not end in **-s**.	some **animals'** habitats the **women's** hats

Use a **possessive adjective** to tell who owns something.

| **my puppy** | **your mother** | **her cat** | **his hat** |
| **its wings** | **our house** | **their skates** | |

Write the correct form of the possessive nouns and adjectives.

1. A _____ *man's* _____ exotic pet escaped! He was lucky to find
   (man's, mans')
   _____________ pet in the park.

2. _____________ friends dumped _____________ terrarium
   (Mine, My)   (their, they're)
   plants in the yard. The _____________ mistake could have been
                          (children's, childrens')
   harmful. We must work together to solve _______ problems.
                                           (us, our)

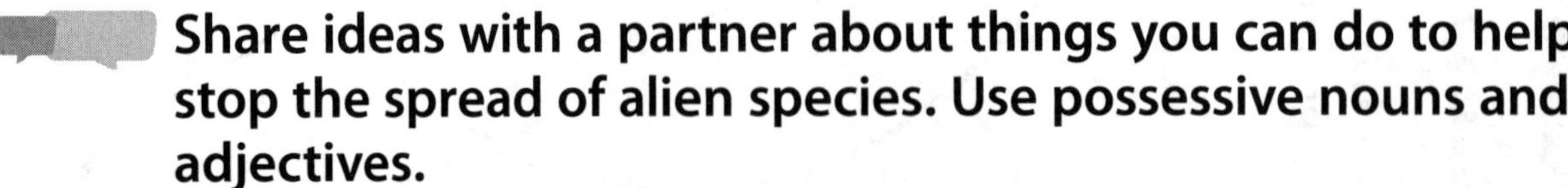

Share ideas with a partner about things you can do to help stop the spread of alien species. Use possessive nouns and adjectives.

Putting **Ants** on **Ice**

by Kayla Handler

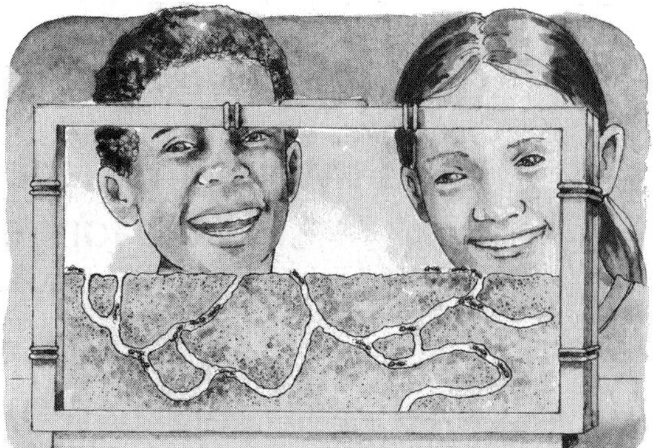

Question: How do changes in air temperature affect ants' movements?

Hypothesis: Ants will move faster in an environment with cold air than in an environment with warm air.

Materials: ant habitat, refrigerator

Procedure:

1. Observe how fast the ants in the ant habitat move at room temperature.
2. Put the ant habitat in the refrigerator for 10 minutes.
3. Observe how fast the ants move after 10 minutes in the refrigerator.
4. Leave the ant habitat at room temperature for 10 minutes.
5. Observe how fast the ants move after 10 minutes at room temperature again.

Results: At room temperature, the ants were lively and moved quickly. After I took them out of the refrigerator, the ants were slow and inactive. After another 10 minutes, the ants moved as quickly as before.

Analysis: I predicted that ants would move more quickly in an environment with cold air than in an environment with warm air. However, when I put them in the refrigerator, the ants moved more slowly. After 10 minutes at room temperature, they moved more quickly again. My hypothesis was incorrect.

Conclusion: Ants' movements change according to the air temperature of their environment.

Snails! Who Needs Them?

by Kayla Handler

Question: What contributes to the balance of an ecosystem?

Hypothesis: In science class we learned that an ecosystem will no longer be balanced if something disturbs it. We also saw a video that explained that snails eat algae and decompose waste and dead plants and animals. When snails are part of an ecosystem, they help the plants and fish by keeping the water clean and clear. So, I think if I remove snails from an aquarium, the tank will get dirty.

Materials: large glass tank, gravel, dropper, hand lens, measuring cup, algae, water, plants, three guppies (small fish), Elodea (plant), two pond snails

Procedure:

1. Put one cup of gravel into the tank and pour in water until the tank is about ¾ full.

2. Add two plants to the water.

3. Put four droppers full of algae in the water.

4. Place the guppies and snails in the tank. Examine the animals and plants and observe how clean the aquarium is. Write your observations.

5. Observe the tank every day and record your observations. After three days, remove the snails and place them in a separate tank with food and water.

6. Continue to observe the aquarium every day for four days and record your observations.

▲ An aquarium is a great v
observe a complete eco

Snails! Who Needs Them? (continued)

Results:

Day 1: The water is clear.

Day 2: The water is clear. I observed the fish eating the plants, but I have not noticed the snails' eating habits. I cannot see the algae without a magnifying glass.

Day 3: The water is still clean. The snail and fish populations are the same.

Day 4: I removed the snails this morning. I wonder what will happen!

Day 5: The water is not as clear today. I still need a magnifying glass to see the algae.

Day 6: The water looks dirty. I don't even need a magnifying glass to see the algae.

Day 7: There is even more algae today than yesterday. The tank looks dirty.

Analysis: Removing the snails threw the whole ecosystem out of balance. My hypothesis was correct.

Conclusion: Taking away a species disturbs the balance of an ecosystem.

◀ Without snails to clean up the environment, the aquarium ecosystem is out of balance.

Edit and Proofread

Choose the Editing and Proofreading Marks you need to correct the passage. Look for the following:

- correct order of adjectives
- correct formation of possessive nouns
- correct usage of possessive adjectives

Editing and Proofreading Marks

∧	Add.
℘	Take out.
⟲∧	Move to here.
∨̇	Add apostrophe.
∿	Transpose.

Ahmeds favorite topic in science class is the ocean. His interest in the ocean and their inhabitants began when he was a child. Her goal is to become a marine successful ecologist. Both his parents are scientists and its careers have inspired him.

The oceans' ecosystem is so vast that at first Ahmed didn't know where to start studying. He asked his mother what to do, and your idea was to start with one animal. He chose the blue whale. He learned that this blue-gray long creature is the largest mammal that has ever lived on Earth. Their dimensions astounded him. The blue whales length extends to about 100 feet. Our weight can soar to 160 tons!

Ahmed often tells his mom, "Thanks for telling me its idea. It has made her goal of learning all about the ocean easier!"

A Show for the Birds

Grammar Rules: Possessives

A **possessive noun** tells who owns something • It uses an apostrophe. • It matches the number of owners.	The bird's nest is new. The three birds' nests are new.
A **possessive adjective** replaces the owners name. • It does *not* use an apostrophe. • It matches the number of owners.	Nara has a pet bird. Her bird is a canary. Nara and Mina's pet bird is a canary. Their bird is a parakeet.

Underline the word that correctly completes each sentence.

1. The (birds/bird's) give (our/our's) family a lot of laughs.
2. (Your/Your's) bird also is funny as it plays (its/it's/its') games.
3. We could have talent show with all the (birds/birds').
4. If Michael brings (his/his') parrot, the (parrots/parrot's) whistle might win.
5. However, your (birds'/bird's) act is impressive, too.

 **Tell a partner about a pet you or a friend has. Use possessive nouns and adjectives to tell about the pet**

Treasure Hunters

Make a concept map with the answers to the Big Question: Why do we seek treasure?

Name ____ Date ___________________

Finding a Treasure

Complete a character map for a favorite character. In the top squares, note the important events in the story, and the important relationships the character has. In the bottom squares, explain how the character changes and why.

Character Map

Events	Relationships

Character ____

Beginning	Middle	End

 Use your character map to tell your partner how and why your character changed.

Indefinite Adjective Tic-Tac-Toe

1. **Play with a partner. Take turns selecting an indefinite adjective from the word box.**
2. **Use the indefinite adjective in a sentence. If your partner agrees that you used it correctly, put an *X* or an *O* on the tic-tac-toe grid. If not, do not make a mark, and allow your partner to take a turn.**
3. **Take turns playing until someone gets three *X*'s or three *O*'s in a row.**
4. **Play the game three more times.**

How Many		How Much	
many	several	much	not much
some	few	some	a little
a lot of	no	a lot of	no

Edit and Proofread

Choose the Editing and Proofreading Marks you need to correct the passage. Look for correct usage of the following:

- possessive adjectives
- indefinite adjectives
- subject pronouns

Editing and Proofreading Marks

∧	Add.
ℐ	Take out.
⊂⊃∧	Move to here.
∧̦	Add comma.
⊙	Add period.

Today I went to a birthday party for Kim, a girl in ~~his~~ my class. I was

nervous because I am new at school. The other kids have known each

other for much years. You are really good friends.

Fortunately, the party was many fun! Kim's mom had arranged a

scavenger hunt. He gave pairs of us a list of clues. Their buddy was a

boy named Sunil. He made a great team!

Some clues were pretty hard. One clue said to take five steps

north. Sunil said, "No problem—this way is north." She is so good at

directions! It didn't take us many time to find the treasure. Best of all,

it had forgotten all about being nervous.

Predict the Answer

Read each question about "Treasure Island." Choose the best answer.

Sample

1 Who hid in the barrel and overheard the sailors talking?

- ● Jim
- Ⓑ Long John Silver
- Ⓒ Trelawney
- Ⓓ Smollett

2 When Jim is hiding in the barrel, what does he learn about Long John Silver?

- Ⓐ He is a cook.
- Ⓑ He is a pirate.
- Ⓒ He tells interesting stories.
- Ⓓ He has a wooden leg.

3 Who hid the treasure in the cave?

- Ⓐ Jim
- Ⓑ Trelawney
- Ⓒ Ben
- Ⓓ Long John Silver

 **Tell a partner how you used the strategy to answer the questions.**

Character Map

"Treasure Island"

Complete the character map to tell how Jim changes in the play.

Character Map

Events		Relationships
joining the treasure hunt		Dr. Livesey Long John Silver

Jim

Beginning	Middle	End
boyish but brave		

Use your character map to retell the story to a partner and explain how Jim changed.

"Treasure Island"

Expression is how you use your voice to express feeling. Use this passage to practice reading with proper expression.

JIM *[enters from offstage, alone and out of breath]*: I think	11
I've lost them. *[hopeless]* I was foolish. Why didn't I stay with	23
my friends? *[points upstage]* There's a cave! I'll hide there!	33
[JIM goes into the cave. BEN GUNN enters the cave from offstage.]	45
JIM and **BEN** *[surprised]*: Oh!	50
BEN: Are you real, boy? Who are you?	58
JIM: I'm Jim Hawkins. Who are you?	65
BEN: I'm Ben Gunn. For three years I've been alone here!	76
JIM: Were you shipwrecked?	80
BEN: No, I was marooned, left here to die. I stayed alive by	93
trapping wild goats. What I wouldn't give for a bit of toasted	105
cheese! Tell me true, boy! Is that Flint's ship out there?	116

From "Treasure Island," page 373

Intonation

1 ☐ Does not read with feeling.

2 ☐ Reads with some feeling, but does not match content.

3 ☐ Reads with appropriate feeling for most content.

4 ☐ Reads with appropriate feeling for all content.

Accuracy and Rate Formula

Use the formula to measure a reader's accuracy and rate while reading aloud.

_____________	−	_____________	=	_____________
words attempted in one minute		number of errors		words correct per minute (wcpm)

Gardens

Grammar Rules: Adjectives

Possessive adjectives come before a noun. They show who possesses, or owns, something.	<u>My</u> plants grow well. <u>Their</u> plants do not grow well. <u>His</u> plants have pretty flowers.
Indefinite adjectives also come before a noun. Use these when you are not sure of the number.	<u>Many</u> people like plants. <u>Most</u> people like growing plants. <u>Several</u> friends grow plants.

Write the correct adjective to complete each sentence.

1. Mark and Pedro planted a community garden. _____________ garden grows fast. [His/Their]
2. We also started a garden. We love _____________ new fresh vegetables. [our/her]
3. My sister cooks all our meals with vegetables from the garden. _____________ meals are delicious. [Most/Their]
4. Tai has made desserts from _____________ fruits that grow there too. [your/several]
5. I planted corn. _____________ corn grew tall. [My/Many]

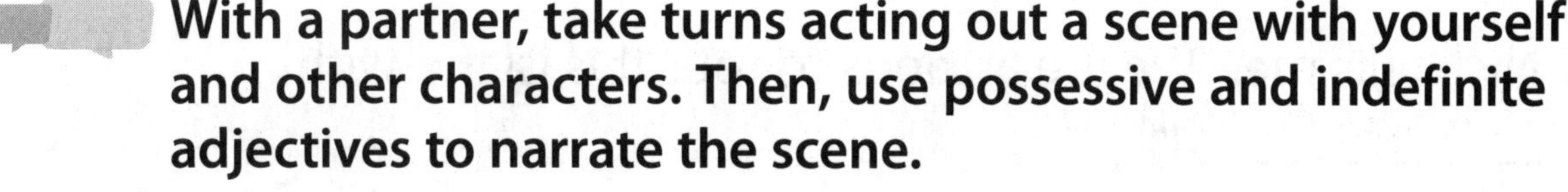

With a partner, take turns acting out a scene with yourself and other characters. Then, use possessive and indefinite adjectives to narrate the scene.

Grammar: Game

Visiting with Object Pronouns

Directions:

1. With your partner, copy each of the eight sentence frames below onto separate index cards.
2. Shuffle all the sentence cards and stack them face down.
3. Take turns turning over a card and completing the sentence with an object pronoun. Your object pronoun should refer to the underlined word in the first sentence. Read your completed sentence aloud.
4. If your partner agrees that your sentence is correct, keep the card. If not, replace the card at the bottom of the stack.
5. Play until no cards remain in the stack. The player with the most cards at the end of the game wins.

____

1. The <u>ship</u> is nearing the shore. I will meet _______________ .

2. I see my <u>cousins</u> on board, and I wave to _______________ .

3. They came to see our island and visit <u>our family</u>. They will stay with _______________ .

4. "<u>Tyra and Nick</u>, I'm happy to see _______________ ," I say.

5. They hug _______________ and say <u>I</u> have grown taller.

6. <u>Nick</u> heads toward the bus stop, and we follow _______________ .

7. <u>Tyra</u> climbs onto the bus that goes by our house. I hop on after _______________ .

8. Nick tells <u>me</u>, "We are anxious to tour this island with _______________ !"

Reflexive Pronoun Race

Directions:

1. Take turns with a partner. Player 1 flips a coin. Move one space for heads. Move two spaces for tails.
2. Read aloud the word on the space where you land and use the word in a sentence. If your partner agrees that your sentence is correct, stay where you are. If not, move back to your space at the beginning of your turn.
3. The first player to reach the finish wins.

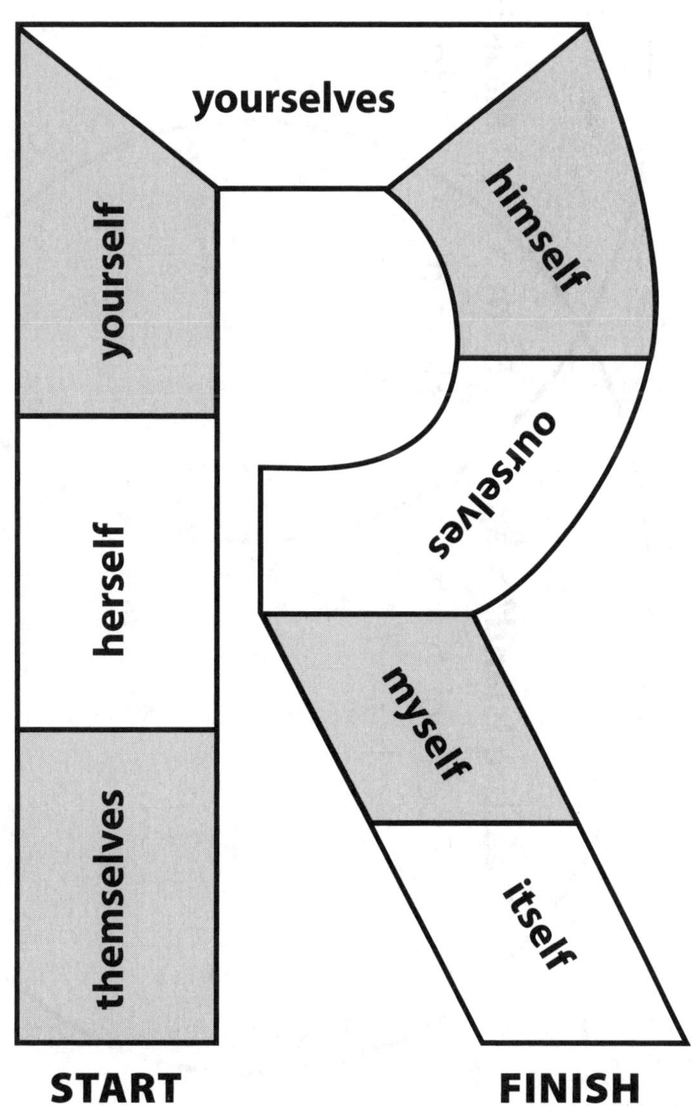

Compare Texts

Complete the Venn diagram to compare the treasure maps in the selections.

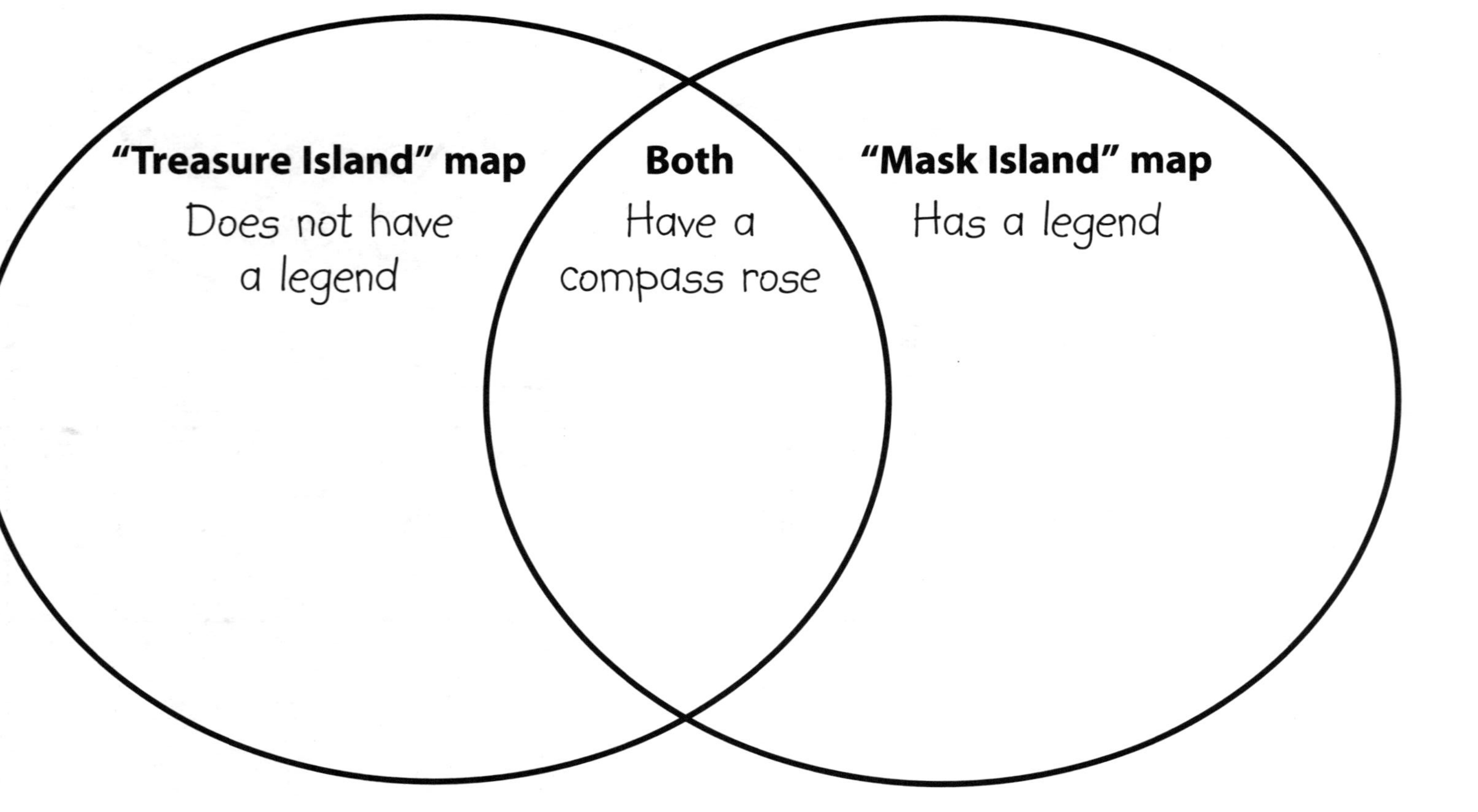

Share your Venn diagram with a partner. Talk about the features each map has.

A Tasty Treasure Hunt

Grammar Rules Pronoun Agreement

A pronoun can take the place of a noun.
The chart shows which pronoun to use.

Subject Pronouns		Object Pronouns		Pronouns that Name the Same Noun Twice	
Singular	**Plural**	**Singular**	**Plural**	**Singular**	**Plural**
I	we	me	us	myself	ourselves
you	you	you	you	yourself	yourselves
she	they	her	them	herself	themselves
he		him		himself	
it		it		itself	

Read the paragraph. Replace the word or words under the line with the correct pronoun.

My little brother Jake likes pirates. _____He_____ reads about __________
_____ (Jake) _____ (pirates)

all the time. My mom and I are planning a surprise for __________ .
(Jake)

__________ will hide a treasure. Then we will make a treasure map.
(Mom and I)

Jake will use __________ to find the treasure. Mom helped __________
(map) (I)

draw the map. But I hid the present by __________ . I hope Jake
(I)

shares __________ with __________ . The treasure is a box full of his
(present) (Mom and Me)

favorite cookies. Mom and I made them __________ .
(Mom and I)

Talk with a partner. Tell about a "treasure" you could hide for a friend. Notice the pronouns you use as you talk.

Today Is the Day! by Margaret Schultz

SCENE ONE
[**SETTING:** *Crew members stand on a Spanish ship near Florida in 1625.*]

ALFONSO, crew member: Enrique is looking for *Nuestra Señora de Atocha* now, Captain. No one has seen it since it sank in 1622. I hope we find it!

CAPTAIN MELIÁN, captain of the ship: He'd better hurry! We have to return to port soon, and I want that treasure!

ALFONSO: [*pointing*] Look, sir!

[ENRIQUE, a diver, *comes to the surface of the water*]

MELIÁN: Enrique, what did you see underwater?

ENRIQUE: [*waving coins*] I found gold coins, but I didn't see the *Atocha*!

ALFONSO: [*holding up a coin*] When we find the *Atocha*, we'll be rich!

MELIÁN: [*snatching the coin from Alfonso*] You'll get your share—once I take mine, first!

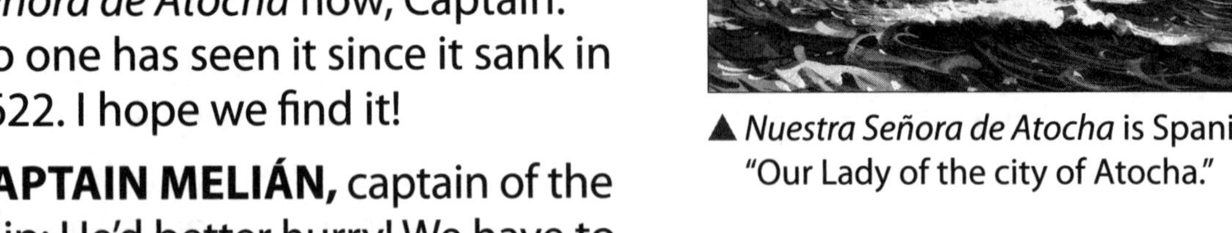

▲ *Nuestra Señora de Atocha* is Spanish for "Our Lady of the city of Atocha."

Character	Information from the text	Information from the performance
Alfonso		
Captain Melián		

Today Is the Day! (continued)

SCENE TWO
[**SETTING:** MEL FISHER, a treasure hunter, and EUGENE LYON, a historian, sit in the cabin of MEL's boat in the 1970s.]

EUGENE LYON: Unfortunately for Captain Melián, he uncovered lots of coins but never found the actual ship. I think he was really close, so shouldn't we be looking in the same place? According to Melián's map, we are nowhere near the *Atocha*!

▲ The treasure on the *Atocha* was worth a fortune—more than 400 million US dollars!

MEL FISHER: Eugene, are you saying that all this time we have misjudged where the ship disappeared?

EUGENE: [*excitedly*] Yes! All along we thought the ship sank near this cluster of islands [*points at the map*]. But if I understand this map correctly, we need to look near these islands! [*He jabs at a different place on the map.*]

MEL: [*firmly*] Let's do it! I've already put a tremendous amount of time and money into looking for the *Atocha*. It's unthinkable to give up now!

EUGENE: [*eagerly*] We are going to be rich!

MEL: [*laughs*] It's true that the treasure is worth about four hundred million dollars, but I also want to find the ship because it's an incredible piece of history, and I want to display it in a museum so everyone can share it! Tomorrow we will start looking near those other islands.

Today Is the Day! (continued)

SCENE THREE

[**SETTING:** MEL and EUGENE are on the deck of a boat in 1985.]

EUGENE: [*discouraged*] Sometimes I think finding that ship is impossible! I thought we would have uncovered it by now.

MEL: [*encouraging*] Don't worry, Eugene, we will find it. Today is the day! I will never stop looking!

[*The radio in front of MEL crackles.*]

KANE FISHER: [*from the radio speaker*] Dad! Can you hear me?

MEL: [*scrambles to pick up the receiver*] Yes, what is it, Kane?

KANE: Dad, we found the *Atocha*! We finally found it!

EUGENE: [*shocked*] I can't believe it! [*jumps excitedly*]

MEL: [*laughing*] You got it, Eugene—today really *is* the day!

Write what you learn from the text and from the performance.

Character	Information from the text	Information from the performance
Mel Fisher		
Eugene Lyon		

Edit and Proofread

Choose the editing and proofreading marks you need to correct the passage. Look for correct usage of the following:

- object pronouns
- reflexive pronouns
- subject pronouns

Editing and Proofreading Marks

∧	Add.
℘	Take out.
⟳∧	Move to here.
⋀	Add comma.
⊙	Add period.

Mom cooled ~~himself~~ *herself* with a magazine, waving it in front of her

face. She put them down and sighed. "It's too hot today," you said.

"Let's go to the beach."

Mom didn't have to convince us! We piled yourselves into the

car and headed for the shore. My little brother yapped all the way. I

glared at her sharply. "Be quiet!" I said.

When we got there, they ran to the ocean. We flung myself in the

cool water. Mom had a picnic, and I helped me spread it out on a

blanket. Later I played a pirate game with my little brother. She cried

when he couldn't find the buried treasure. So I drew a treasure map

that he could follow.

Grammer: Reteach

Musical Students

Grammar Rules: Pronouns

Subject pronouns replace a noun in a sentence.	Ava is a beautiful singer. She has the best voice.
Object pronouns come after an action verb or a preposition.	Rafael sings to friends. The friends love the songs he sings to them.
Reflexive pronouns end with *-self* or *-selves*. They refer to the subject in a sentence.	Ava taught herself how to sing.
Nouns and pronouns agree because they refer to the same person or thing.	Ray and Max walk home. They sing the whole way.

Read the sentences below. Circle pronouns and draw an arrow to nouns they agree with.

1. Mrs. Lee teaches music. She has the most popular class.

2. Tomorrow, the parents will come listen. They are excited.

3. All the students are proud of themselves.

4. Ava and Rafael practice a lot with friends who practice with them.

5. Rafael is especially pleased with himself.

With a partner, discuss the music you like. Use subject, object, and reflexive pronouns.

Make a Time Line

Make a time line to show the steps you took to find a lost object.

Time Line

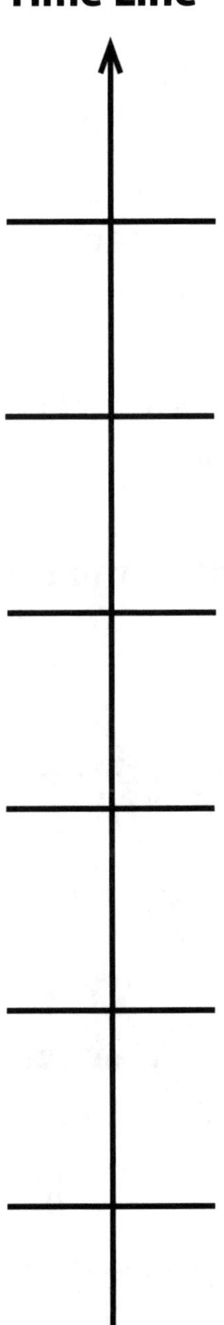

 **Use your time line to tell a partner about your search for a lost object.**

Grammar: Game

Demonstrate Your Knowledge!

Directions:

1. With a partner, cut out the first three rows of word cards and spread them out face up on a table.

2. Cut out the last two rows of cards. Use colored pencils or crayons to draw the item or items named on each card. Spread the picture cards on the table beside the word cards.

3. Take turns choosing four or more cards to make a sentence. For each sentence, use *this, that, these,* or *those* as a demonstrative adjective or a demonstrative pronoun.

4. If your partner correctly identifies how you used the word (as a demonstrative adjective or as a demonstrative pronoun), he or she gets one point.

5. Play until you have each made at least six different sentences. The player with more points at the end wins.

this	that	these	those
is	are	a	.
rusty	silver	gold	cracked
(plate)	(plates)	(ring)	(rings)
(sword)	(swords)	(coin)	(coins)

Edit and Proofread

Choose the Editing and Proofreading Marks you need to correct the passage. Look for the following:

- demonstrative adjectives
- indefinite adjectives
- demonstrative pronouns

Editing and Proofreading Marks

∧	Add.
℘	Take out.
⌒∧	Move to here.
∧,	Add comma.
⊙	Add period.

This
"~~That~~ place sure is dark," I thought as we entered the cave. "This ∧ sounds like a bat flying overhead." These was my first outing with the Young Explorers Club. I didn't think trip this would be so creepy!

Inside the cave, Mr. Madsen pointed up to some long spears hanging from the cave ceiling. "This are stalactites," he said. Then we crowded close around formations rising up from the cave floor like castle towers. Mr. Madsen explained, "Those formations are called stalagmites. That are famous because they are so tall."

When he pointed to an exit sign and said, "Let's go way," I was relieved. I was happy to get out of this cave!

Test-Taking Strategy Practice

Write Fluid Sentences

Directions: Read each pair of sentences. Then read the questions. Choose the best answer.

Sample

> We found Spanish coins in many sizes.
>
> We found Spanish coins in many shapes.
>
> **1** Which is the best way to combine the sentences?
>
> Ⓐ We found Spanish coins in many sizes and many shapes.
>
> ● We found Spanish coins in many sizes and shapes.
>
> Ⓒ We found Spanish coins in many sizes and we found them in many shapes.
>
> Ⓓ We found coins in many sizes and shapes from Spain.

> The ship's treasures sank into the ocean.
>
> The ship's treasures disappeared into the ocean.
>
> **2** Which is the best way to combine the sentences?
>
> Ⓐ The ship's treasures sank into the ocean and the treasures disappeared in the ocean.
>
> Ⓑ The ship's treasures sank and disappeared.
>
> Ⓒ The ship's treasures sank into the ocean and disappeared.
>
> Ⓓ The ship's treasures sank. They disappeared into the ocean.

Tell a partner how you used the strategy to answer the questions.

     PM6.21

Time Line

"Real Pirates"

Complete the time line to tell the sequence of events in "Real Pirates."

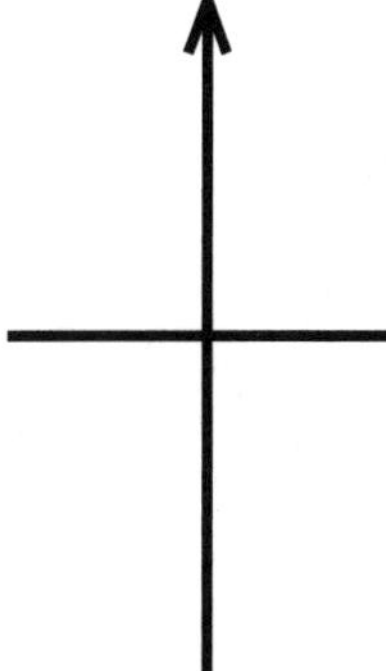

In 1715 the slave ship *Whydah* was built.

Captain Prince took the ship to Africa.

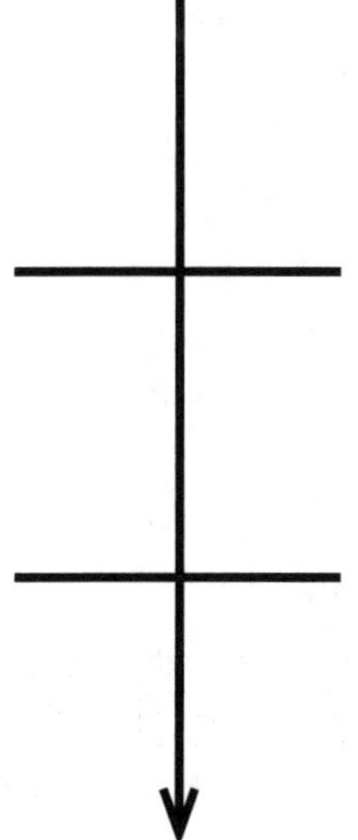

Use your time line to retell the article to a partner.

"Real Pirates"

Use this passage to practice reading with proper phrasing.

After capturing the *Whydah*, the pirates sailed north, robbing 9
more rich ships on the way. 15

Then the *Whydah* was struck by a storm off Cape Cod on 27
the night of April 26, 1717. Strong winds drove the *Whydah* onto 39
a sandbar just 500 feet from shore. The ship was slammed by 51
waves up to twenty feet high. Soon, the mainmast snapped. 61
The *Whydah* was pushed off the sandbar and capsized. 70

There were 145 men and at least one boy aboard the *Whydah*. 82
Only two made it to shore alive. The rest died in the dark, cold water. 97

The *Whydah's* riches quickly sank. They disappeared in the 106
shifting sands of the Cape. There they stayed for nearly three 117
hundred years. 119

From "Real Pirates," page 402

Intonation

1 ☐ Rarely pauses while reading the text.   3 ☐ Frequently pauses at appropriate points in the text.

2 ☐ Occasionally pauses while reading the text.   4 ☐ Consistently pauses at all appropriate points in the text.

Accuracy and Rate Formula
Use the formula to measure a reader's accuracy and rate while reading aloud.

words attempted in one minute	−	number of errors	=	words correct per minute (wcpm)

Grammar: Reteach

Bird Watching

Grammar Rules: Demonstratives

A **demonstrative pronoun** matches the noun it replaces. It tells if the noun is near or far.	This is an old dog. (one) These are old dogs. (plural) This is a nice dog Kennel. (near) Those are nice dog Kennels. (far)
A **demonstrative adjective** matches the noun it describes. It also tells if the noun is near or far.	This puppy is cute. (one) These puppies are cute. (plural) This puppy is mine. (near) That puppy across the street is his. (far)

Circle the word that correctly completes each sentence.

1. I love (this/these) five baby birds.
2. (This/Those) boys will help the birds by giving them seeds.
3. All the birds eat the seeds, except (that/those) one.
4. (That/These) taste good to most of the birds.
5. (This/Those) is nice to watch.

Tell a partner about pets and what they like. Use demonstrative pronouns and demonstrative adjectives.

Grammar: Game

Pronoun Picture

Directions:

1. With your partner, think of a simple picture you can draw with six lines, such as a ship, a treasure chest, or a tree, but don't draw it yet.

2. Take turns. Circle the indefinite pronoun in a sentence below. Then underline the correct form of the verb in parentheses and write it on the line to complete that sentence.

3. If your partner agrees that you circled the indefinite pronoun and completed the sentence with the correct verb, add one line to the picture.

4. If not, your partner corrects the sentence and adds a line to the picture.

5. After all sentences are complete, your picture will be complete, too!

---

1. Each of the sailors _________ minor injuries after the pirates attacked the Sea Queen. (have/has)

2. Someone on the Sea Queen _________ an island in the distance, and wonders if a doctor lives there. (sees/see)

3. However, nobody _________ the rowboat there that day. (take/takes)

4. Something on the Sea Queen _________ damaged in the fight. (were/was)

5. Nothing _________ the sailors more than damage to their ship. (worry/worries)

6. Everybody _________ to fix the damage before going to the island. (agrees/agree)

PM6.25

Who Does What?

Directions:

1. With your team, cut apart the indefinite pronoun cards on this page. Set them aside.

2. Then collaborate to write four sentences. Have each sentence begin with a singular indefinite pronoun and include a present tense verb. Here are some examples:

   Somebody wants to explore the desert.

   Nobody in my family likes peppermint.

3. Play with another team. Combine your indefinite pronoun cards, shuffle them, and spread them face down on a table. Then exchange the papers on which you have written your sentences.

4. Team 1 draws a card and rewrites the first sentence using the plural indefinite pronoun on the card and paying attention to the verb form. Team 1 reads its new sentence aloud.

5. If Team 2 agrees that the sentence is correct, Team 1 gets a point.

6. Then Team 2 takes a turn.

7. Play continues until all the sentences have been changed. The team with more points wins.

Both	Few	Many	Several

Compare Media Texts

Use the comparison chart to compare "La Belle Shipwreck" to a blog.

Feature	Web Article	Blog
Title	"La Belle Shipwreck"	
Name of author	Texas Beyond History	
Date when written	no	
Is the text in sections?		
Are there pictures?		
Does the information change often?		
Are there mostly facts or mostly opinions?		
Are there links to other articles and Web sites or definitions?		

 **Take turns with a partner. Ask each other questions about the features of Web articles and blogs.**

The Treasure Is Yours

Grammar Rules Possessive Pronouns

Use **possessive pronouns** to show that someone owns something.

Possessive Pronouns	mine	yours	his	hers	ours	theirs

A possessive pronoun does not come before a noun.

A possessive pronoun stands alone.

Answer each question with a possessive pronoun.

1. Are these their ships?   No, the ships are not __*theirs*__ .

2. Is this La Salle's ship?   Yes, this ship is __________ .

3. Is this our shipwreck?   Yes, this shipwreck is __________ .

4. Is this the woman's shoe?   Yes, this shoe is __________ .

5. Are these your tools?   No, those tools are __________ .

6. Is that your treasure?   Yes, this treasure is __________ .

 Ask a partner questions about classroom objects. Use language frames: Whose __________ is this? Whose __________ are these? Have your partner use possessive pronouns to answer the questions. Then switch roles.

Mark-Up Reading

The *Mary Rose*

Ship's History | About the Exhibit | Links | Contact Us

Ship's History

- **Henry's Favorite Ship**
- **Rediscovering the Ship**
- **A Museum for the *Mary Rose***

Henry's Favorite Ship

On July 19, 1545, <u>King Henry VIII</u> of England watched with admiration as the *Mary Rose* sailed away. Historians believe that the *Mary Rose* was the king's favorite ship because he had named it after his sister, <u>Mary</u>, and his family's symbol, the rose. Even though the ship had a pretty name, its job was not so pretty. The *Mary Rose* was a massive wooden <u>battleship</u>. Henry was at <u>war with the French</u>.

The *Mary Rose* had a number of large guns that could damage opposing ships. The guns were below deck, and the crew would fire them through windows, called <u>gun ports</u>. When the crew was not using the guns, they kept the gun ports shut to keep the seawater out. But on this day, because the *Mary Rose* was headed into battle, the gun ports were wide open.

▲ The *Mary Rose* carried heavy cannons.

The wind was blowing hard. As the crew of the *Mary Rose* tried to make a complicated turn, the ship started to lean too far to one side. Since the gun ports on that side of the ship were open, water flooded rapidly into the hold. Henry watched with horror as his favorite ship and its crew quickly sank to the bottom of the sea.

Mark-Up Reading

Ship's History

- **Henry's Favorite Ship**
- **Rediscovering the Ship**
- **A Museum for the *Mary Rose***

Rediscovering the Ship

Hundreds of years passed before anyone found the wreck of the *Mary Rose*. There was a reason why it was so hard to find: strong currents carried mud and silt over the sunken ship, and a layer of clay built up on top of the wreckage. The clay preserved the ship but also made it difficult to spot it on the sea floor.

In 1836, a fisherman's net snagged on something. What was it? A piece of the ship that was sticking out of the clay grabbed the net! The fisherman contacted a diver named <u>John Deane</u>, a diver who used a helmet that allowed him to breathe under water for short periods of time. After bringing up one of the guns from the ship, Deane knew he had found the *Mary Rose*. He collected a few more items but then decided that most of the wreckage was too difficult to bring to the surface.

In the 1960s, an <u>underwater archaeologist</u> named <u>Alexander McKee</u> went in search of the *Mary Rose*. McKee knew that the fisherman and Deane had found the ship more than 100 years before, but he did not know the exact location. Using modern equipment, McKee was able to rediscover the ship. After years of underwater excavation, McKee and his team pulled the entire boat out of the water in 1982. What a feat!

Mark-Up Reading

The *Mary Rose*

Ship's History
- **Henry's Favorite Ship**
- **Rediscovering the Ship**
- **A Museum for the *Mary Rose***

A Museum for the *Mary Rose*

Scientists have examined more than 19,000 artifacts from the ship. They have put the ship and some of the items on display in a <u>museum</u> for the enjoyment of visitors. The exhibition has plates, mugs, board games, shoes, guns, musical instruments, and other items that the crew possessed.

▲ The Mary Rose Museum is in Portsmouth, England.

Instead of the fabulous wealth most treasure hunters hoped to find, only 27 gold coins were found on board. But visitors to the museum come to see a different kind of treasure. They get a glimpse into what life was like for King Henry VIII's sailors in 1545. It is almost like traveling back through time.

Explanation

How I will use blue links in text: ____

How I will use the menu: ____

How I will use the submenu: ____

How I will use the navigation arrows: ____

How the online text features can help me understand the article and more about the topic: ____

Grammar: Grammar and Writing

Edit and Proofread

Choose the editing and proofreading marks you need to correct the passage. Look for correct usage of:

- indefinite pronouns
- possessive pronouns

Editing and Proofreading Marks

∧	Add.
⤶	Take out.
⃝ ∧	Move to here.
∧̦	Add comma.
⊙	Add period.

"Who is your explorer?" my friend Ava asked as we rode the bus home from school. "~~Yours~~ Mine is Henry Hudson."

"Hey!" I said. "My explorer is the same as yours explorer! Both of us has Henry Hudson."

"Cool," Ava said. "Nobody are as lucky as we are! We can write our reports together. Theirs will be really good."

After an hour of work, Ava read my report and I read her. "They're not very good," I said. "Each of us need to do better."

"Well, anything are better than nothing," Ava replied.

Unit 6 | Treasure Hunters

Party Time

Grammar Rules: Pronouns

Indefinite pronouns can replace nouns. They don't give details. They are • singular, such as every<u>one</u>, some<u>one</u>, and no <u>one</u> • or plural, such as both, few, many, and several.	<u>Everyone</u> at the party <u>is</u> happy. <u>No one</u> <u>is</u> unhappy. <u>Someone</u> <u>plays</u> music. <u>Several</u> <u>are</u> singing. <u>Few</u> <u>are</u> leaving early.
Possessive pronouns tell who or what owns something. • They do not have apostrophes.	The decorations are <u>hers</u>. The chips are <u>his</u>. The dog is happy. <u>Its</u> tail wags.

Complete each sentence with the correct singular or plural verb to match the pronoun or with the correct possessive pronoun.

1. Several _______________ excited about the party when they arrive.
2. Anyone _______________ welcomed to help me clean up now.
3. My turtle hid in his tank. _______________ tank is big.
4. Isabel made the decorations. They are _______________ .
5. Miguel brought the chips. They are _______________ .

Tell a partner about a good time you had. Use indefinite and possessive pronouns to describe it.

Name _______________________   Date _______________

Moving Through Space

Make a concept map with the answers to the Big Question:
What does it take to explore space?

PM7.1

Comparing Sports

Make a comparison chart to compare one of the sports on page 427 with another sport.

Comparison Chart

Sport	Where	Goal	Measure Speed

 Use your comparison chart to tell your partner about the two sports.

Grammar: Game

How It's Done!

Adjectives		Adverbs	
swift	tall	rapidly	extremely
slow	speedy	swiftly	fairly
rapid	sluggish	very	really

Choose adjectives and adverbs from the box to complete the sentences. Follow the order shown in parentheses. Use a variety of adjectives and adverbs!

1. The rocket ship is _____________ _____________ . (adverb, adjective)

2. That falcon flies _____________ _____________ . (adverb, adverb)

3. A person can be _____________ _____________ . (adverb, adjective)

4. Snails are _____________ _____________ . (adverb, adjective)

5. The beam of light travels _____________ _____________ . (adverb, adverb).

6. Cheetahs are _____________ _____________ . (adverb, adjective)

7. This ostrich is _____________ _____________ . (adverb, adjective)

8. The meteoroid zooms _____________ _____________ . (adverb, adverb)

Grammar: Grammar and Writing

Edit and Proofread

Choose the editing and proofreading marks you need to correct the passage. Look for correct usage of:

- adverbs
- adjectives

Editing and Proofreading Marks

∧	Add.
ℐ	Take out.
⌐∧	Move to here.
∧,	Add comma.
⊙	Add period.

Ella stood ~~nervous~~ ^nervously^ at the edge of the pool. Every muscle in her body was tensely as she waited for the signal to begin.

"Go!" the coach yelled sudden. She sprang instant into the blue water. Her arms slashed up. They slashed downly. They were like a whirling windmill slicing through the water.

Freestyle was Ella's best stroke, and she was confidently as she sped through the water. The turn was coming up. She swam energetically, got to the wall, and pushed off hardly. She heard the loudly screams of the crowd, but all her concentration was focused on swimming as fast as she could.

The race was near over. She had a few yards to go. Final she slapped her hand on the edge of the pool. A roar rose quick up from the crowd. She had won, she realized excited!

  PM7.4

Read All Choices

Directions: Read each question about "What's Faster Than a Speeding Cheetah?" Choose the best answer.

Sample

1 Which of the following moves the fastest?

- Ⓐ jet
- Ⓑ cheetah
- Ⓒ falcon
- ● rocket

2 The speed of light is one of the few speeds that is __________ .

- Ⓐ slower at high altitudes
- Ⓑ not constant
- Ⓒ constant
- Ⓓ faster in space

3 Why do we have trouble measuring the speeds of animals?

- Ⓐ They do not come with speedometers.
- Ⓑ They are faster than the speed of sound.
- Ⓒ They are hard to see.
- Ⓓ They are faster than the sound of your voice.

 **Tell a partner how you used the strategy to answer the questions.**

"What's Faster Than a Speeding Cheetah?"

Make a comparison chart for "What's Faster Than a Speeding Cheetah?"

Animal or Object	How it Moves	Fastest Speed	Record
ostrich	runs on two legs	72 km (45 mi) per hour	fastest animal with two legs
cheetah	runs on four legs	113 km (70 mi) per hour	fastest land animal
peregrine falcon			
jet plane			

Use your comparison chart to tell a partner how the animals and objects are alike and different.

"What's Faster Than a Speeding Cheetah?"

Intonation is the rise and fall in the pitch or tone of your voice as you read aloud. Use this passage to practice reading with proper intonation.

Hold on a minute. There's something much faster than even 10

the fastest meteoroid. It's something you see all the time. 20

Just push the switch on a flashlight. Instantly, a light beam 31

will flash out at the amazing speed of 299,338 kilometers per 42

second (186,000 miles per second). 47

That's thousands of times faster than a meteoroid. At that speed, 58

a beam of light could circle Earth more than seven times in one second. 72

Most scientists believe that nothing can travel through space 81

faster than light. Who would have thought that the fastest traveling 92

thing in the whole universe could come out of something small 103

enough to hold in your hand? 109

From "What's Faster Than a Speeding Cheetah?" pages 440–441.

Intonation

1 ☐ Does not change pitch.

2 ☐ Changes pitch, but does not match content.

3 ☐ Changes pitch to match some of the content.

4 ☐ Changes pitch to match all of the content.

Accuracy and Rate Formula

Use the formula to measure a reader's accuracy and rate while reading aloud.

_____________ − _____________ = _____________
words attempted   number of errors   words correct per minute
in one minute   (wcpm)

The Bicycle Race

Grammar Rules: Adverbs

An **adverb** describes a verb. It can come before or after a verb and tells *how, where, when,* or *how often/how much.*

- Many adverbs end in *-ly.*
- An adverb can modify an adjective or another adverb.
- Use an adverb instead of an adjective to tell about a verb.
- Never use an adverb after a form of the verb *to be.*

Miguel pedals his bicycle quickly. (How does he pedal?)

Matt sometimes rests. (How often does he rest?)

Denny bikes very slowly. (How slowly?)

Rosa pedals happily.

Rosa is happy to race.

Read the sentences below. Circle the correct word to complete the sentence.

1. Miguel begins the race (eagerly/eager).
2. Rosa races (easy/easily) to the lead.
3. Denny (careful/carefully) steers on the muddy road.
4. All the racers are (fast/fastly).
5. But, Rosa waits (patiently/patient) at the finish line.
6. She is (proudly/proud) that she won.
7. Rosa will coach the other racers (very/much) (happy/happily) for the next race.

With a partner, discuss the bike race. Take turns using adverbs to describe the different bike riders.

Make a Face!

Draw an oval on a separate sheet of paper. With a partner, take turns drawing a space creature's face by adding one feature, such as eyes or antennae, on the separate paper for each turn. Make your space creature as weird or silly as you like.

Directions:

1. With your partner, take turns completing the sentences. Add *-er* to the adverb in parentheses or use *more* or *less*.

2. If your partner agrees that your sentence is correct, add one feature to the face. If not, your partner corrects the sentence and adds a feature to the face.

3. When the sentences are complete, your Martian will be, too!

---

1. The Martians eat _________________ than pigs. (noisily)

2. They sleep _________________ than bears in winter. (frequently)

3. The creatures on Venus move _________________ than snails. (slow)

4. They jump _________________ than frogs! (high)

5. Some creatures on Jupiter fly _________________ than jets. (fast)

6. Others drift through space _________________ than swans. (gracefully)

Grammar: Game

Match and Make Comparisons

1. Take turns with your partner. Spin the spinner. Look at the letters or words you landed on.

2. Choose an adverb from the box that works with what you landed on. Form a comparison adverb. For example: -est + late = latest.

3. Use your comparison adverb in a sentence.

4. If your partner agrees that your sentence is correct, score 1 point. If not, your partner takes a turn.

5. Continue until all the words in the box have been used correctly to make comparison adverbs. The player with more points at the end is the winner.

| bravely |
| awkwardly |
| late |
| politely |
| quietly |
| fast |

Make a Spinner

1. Put a paper clip over the center of the spinner.
2. Touch the point of a pencil on the middle of the wheel and through the loop of the paper clip.
3. Spin the paper clip to make a spinner.

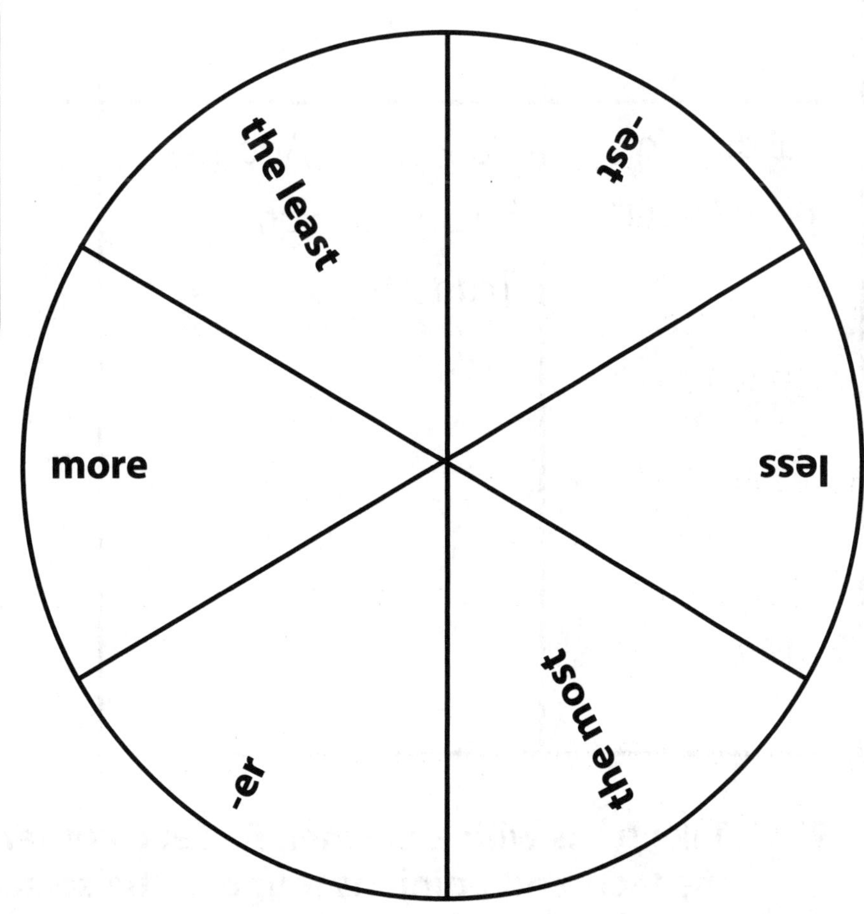

Comparison Chart

Compare Fact and Opinion

Compare facts and opinions in the two selections.

	Facts	**Opinions**
"What's Faster Than a Speeding Cheetah?"		A peregrine falcon is magnificent.
"Building for Space Travel"	Constance Adams helped design TransHAb.	

 **Take turns with a partner. Ask each other questions about the facts and opinions found in the selections.**

For use with TE p. T451a **PM7.11** Unit 7 | Moving Through Space

Exercising in Zero Gravity

Grammar Rules Adverbs

Use **adverbs** to describe and compare actions.

Describe 1 action	soon	carefully	
Compare 2 actions	soon**er**	more careful**ly** than	less careful**ly** than
Compare more than 2 actions	soon**est**	the most careful**ly**	the least careful**ly**

Read each sentence. Write the correct form of the adverb on the line.

1. Every day I enter the gym ___*sooner*___ than my partner.
(soon)

2. I walk in __________ than a gymnast.
(eagerly)

3. I notice that the equipment is attached __________ .
(securely)

4. At first, I ran the __________ of all the astronauts.
(quickly)

5. If I keep practicing, I may one day run the __________ of all.
(fast)

6. Scientists planned TransHab the __________ of any gym.
(carefully)

Pantomime an action an astronaut might do in zero gravity. Have your partner describe or compare your action using an adverb. Then switch roles.

Mark-Up Reading

Dear Astronaut Holmer: *I read that space shuttles have bedrooms. What is it like to sleep on a space shuttle?* — Lukshmi Patel, India

Dear Lukshmi,

Sleeping in space felt very strange at first. It felt odd using a sleeping bag tied to the wall! But otherwise we would float around and bump into things. There is still gravity in a spacecraft, but it's a very weak force. Weak gravity means there's no up or down. Once you're used to it, it's fun to sleep in any direction!

▲ Sometimes astronauts sleep in sleeping bags tied to the walls of the spacecraft.

The light of the Sun also makes sleeping a challenge. We need to sleep eight hours at the end of each work day. However, as the shuttle orbits around Earth, the Sun "rises" every 90 minutes, waking us up too soon. So we wear masks to block out the light while we sleep.

Explanation

Explain how reasons and evidence support the main ideas in the astronaut's answer to Lukshmi:

____

____

____

____

Mark-Up Reading

Dear Astronaut Jamal Holmer:
We learned that space shuttles have exercise rooms. It has to be hard to exercise without gravity! How do you exercise in space?

— Mr. Fletcher's fourth-grade class from California

Dear Class,
Exercising in space is fun and necessary! Imagine what would happen if you never had to walk anywhere or never had to lift heavy objects. Your muscles would get really weak! Luckily, there are plenty of ways to exercise. On the International Space Station, we might use the exercise bike or special equipment that **simulates** lifting weights to keep our muscles strong. Or we might turn somersaults and race from one end of the space station to the other!

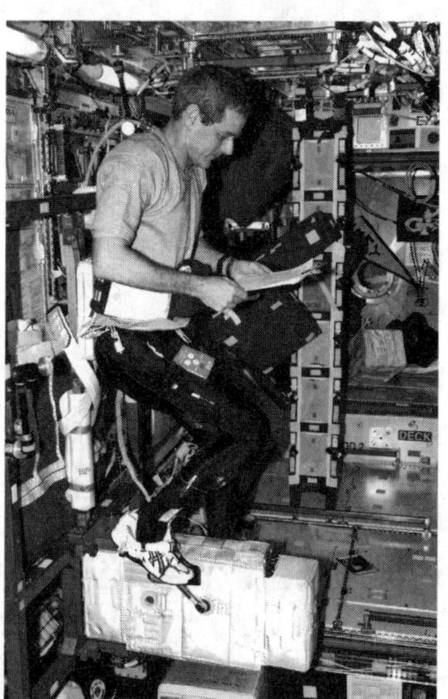

▲ Astronauts need to exercise often to keep their muscles strong.

In Other Words
simulates gives the feeling of

Explanation

Explain how reasons and evidence support the main idea in the astronaut's answer to Mr. Fletcher's class:

____

____

____

____

Edit and Proofread

Choose the Editing and Proofreading Marks you need to correct the passage. Look for correct usage of adverbs with the following.

- *-er* and *-est*
- *more/less* and *the most/the least*
- special forms

Editing and Proofreading Marks

∧	Add.
℘	Take out.
⟲∧	Move to here.
∧,	Add comma.
⊙	Add period.

Do you ever imagine traveling faster than a flash to reach Mars? I have been dreaming about that, but last night I dreamed the most vividly about Mars than I had the night before. In my dream, my rocket ship traveled through space quickly than a real spacecraft. It orbited most well but landed the least gentliest of all the rocket ships arriving on Mars that night.

I stood in a strange landscape. A dust storm blew most fiercely than a blizzard. Huge piles of sand rose higher than a house. Suddenly many small rocks were flying toward me. The one moving the less swiftly of all was coming right at my head. I tried to duck, but I moved more slowlier than a spoon in molasses. Fortunately, then I woke up. I was exhausted. I had slept more badly than any night in my life!

Name ____   Date __________________

Hiking Up the Mountain

Grammar Rules: Adverbs

To compare <u>two actions</u>, add *'er* for many adverbs.	This mountain stands tall<u>er</u> than that one.
Use *more* or *less* for adverbs ending in *'ly*.	That path winds <u>more</u> steep<u>ly</u> than the road.
To compare <u>three or more actions</u>, add *'est* for many adverbs.	This mountain stands the tall<u>est</u> of all the mountains.
Use *the most* or *the least* for adverbs ending in *'ly*.	Max hikes <u>the most</u> eagerly of all his friends.
Special forms: well: better, best badly: worse, worst	I hike <u>well</u>. She hikes <u>better</u> than I do. Ana feels <u>badly</u>. Lara feels <u>worse</u>.

Write the correct word to complete the sentence.

1. Max hikes _____________ than I hike. (better, best)
2. I climb _____________ than he does. (high, higher)
3. Ana walks the most _____________ of all. (slowly, slowliest)
4. Max climbs the _____________ . (more fast, fastest)
5. This hike is _____________ than the last one! (worst, worse)

 **With a partner, take turns using comparison adverbs to compare hiking to another sport.**

Plot of a Story

Make a plot diagram about a favorite story.

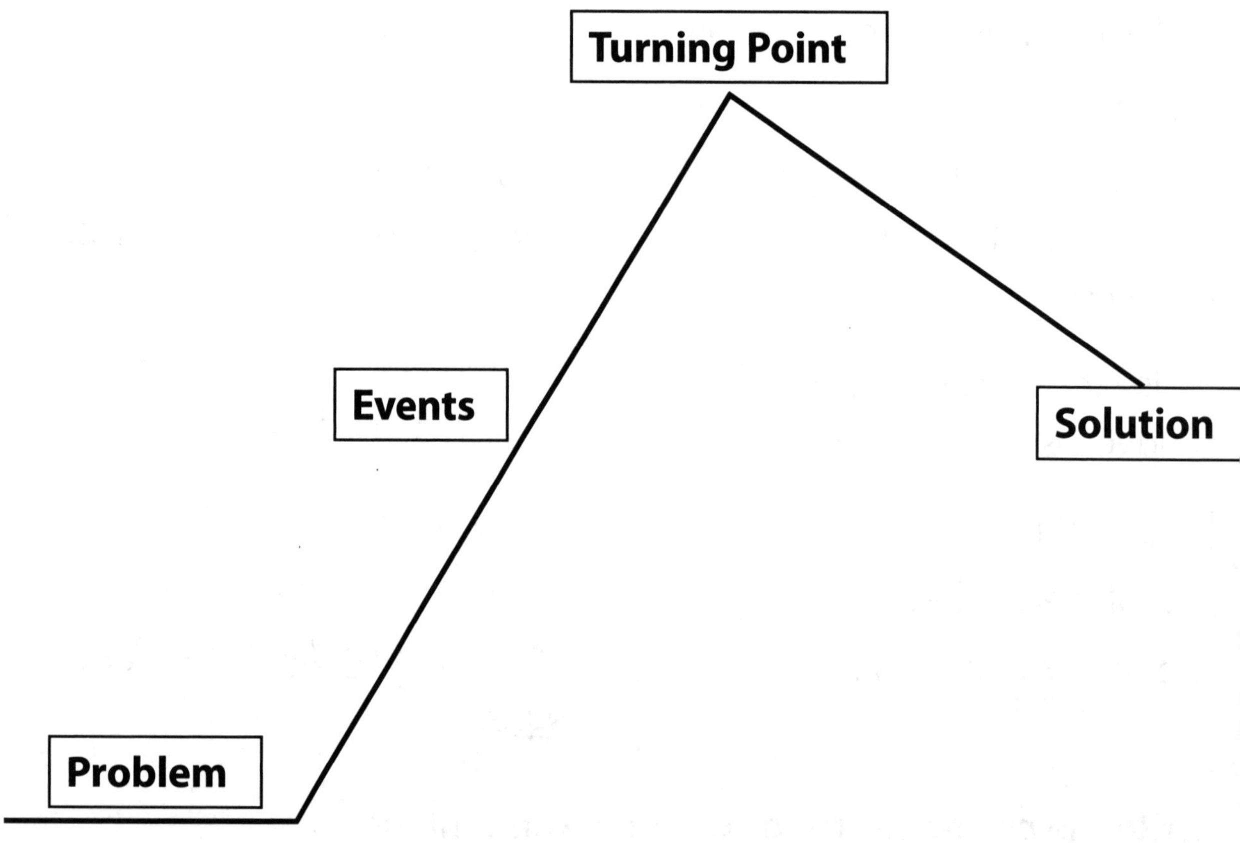

Use the plot diagram to retell your story to a partner.

PM7.17

Relative Adverb Spinner

Directions:

1. **Take turns spinning the spinner.**

2. **Complete the sentence with a dependent clause that begins with the relative adverb** *when.*

3. **Play until you have completed all the sentences. Then play another round!**

Make a Spinner

1. Put a paper clip over the center of the spinner.
2. Touch the point of a pencil on the middle of the wheel and through the loop of the paper clip.
3. Spin the paper clip to make a spinner.

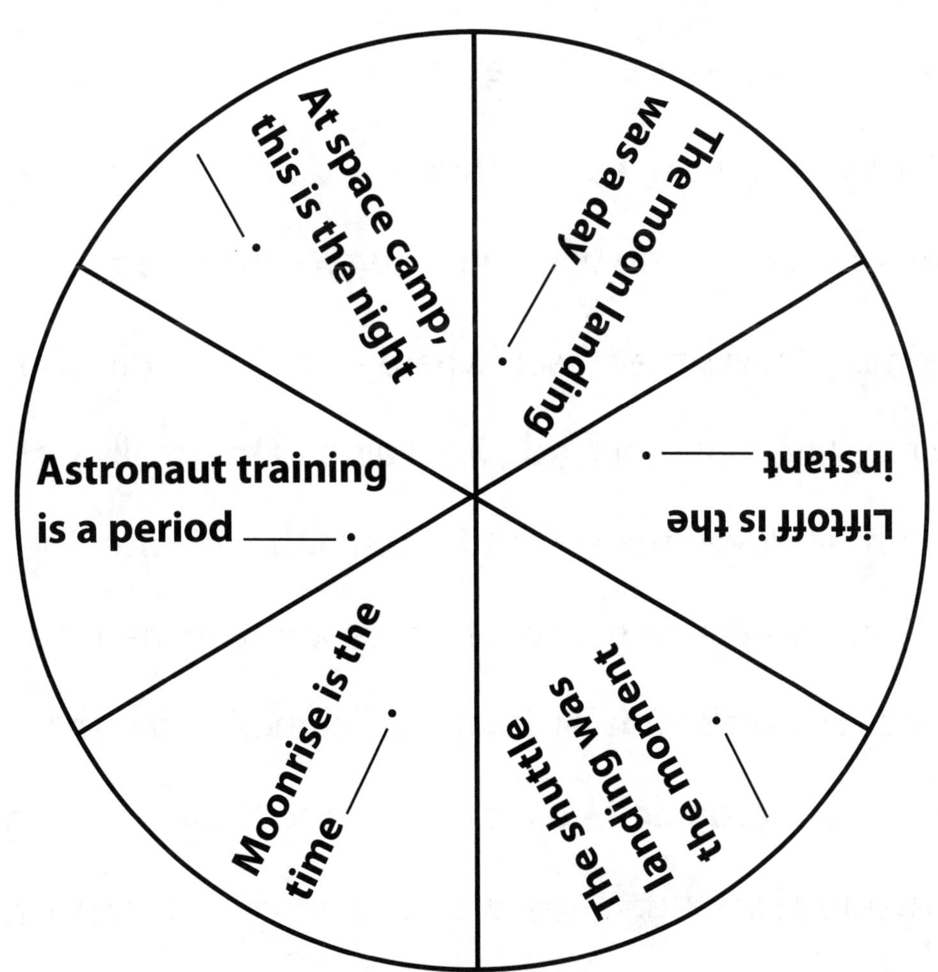

Edit and Proofread

Choose the Editing and Proofreading Marks you need to correct the passage. Look for correct usage of the relative adverbs:

- *when*
- *where*
- *why*

Editing and Proofreading Marks

∧	Add.
℘	Take out.
⟳∧	Move to here.
∧ˌ	Add comma.
⊙	Add period.

"Do you want to go to the space museum?" my cousin Luis asked. "Saturday is the day ~~where~~ when kids get in free."

Luis always has great ideas for things to do. That is the reason when I like to hang around with him. "Sure," I answered.

Free admission was the reason where some kids were there Saturday morning, but other kids, like Luis and me, really wanted to learn stuff. We loved the exhibit for the Hubble Space Telescope. April, 24 1990, was the date where Hubble was launched. And April 24, 2010, was Hubble's 20th birthday! We learned about the place the Hubble space program is directed. It is the NASA Goddard Space Flight Center in Maryland.

Test-Taking Strategy Practice

Read All Choices

Read each question about "The Moon Over Star."
Choose the best answer.

Sample

❶ Why isn't Gramps excited about the moon landing?
- Ⓐ He is working on the tractor in the barn.
- ● He thinks the space program is a waste of money.
- Ⓒ He remembers the first time he saw an airplane.
- Ⓓ He is too tired to watch the moon landing.

❷ Astronaut Neil Armstrong said, "The Eagle has landed." What does this mean?
- Ⓐ An Eagle has landed on the moon.
- Ⓑ An Eagle has landed on the spacecraft.
- Ⓒ The spacecraft has landed on an Eagle.
- Ⓓ The spacecraft has landed on the moon.

❸ Gramps tells Mae to "keep on dreaming." What is Mae's dream?
- Ⓐ watching astronauts on television
- Ⓑ making Gramps proud of her
- Ⓒ going to the moon
- Ⓓ flying an airplane

 **Tell a partner how you used the strategy to answer the questions.**

   PM7.20   **Unit 7** | Moving Through Space

"The Moon Over Star"

Make a plot diagram of "The Moon Over Star."

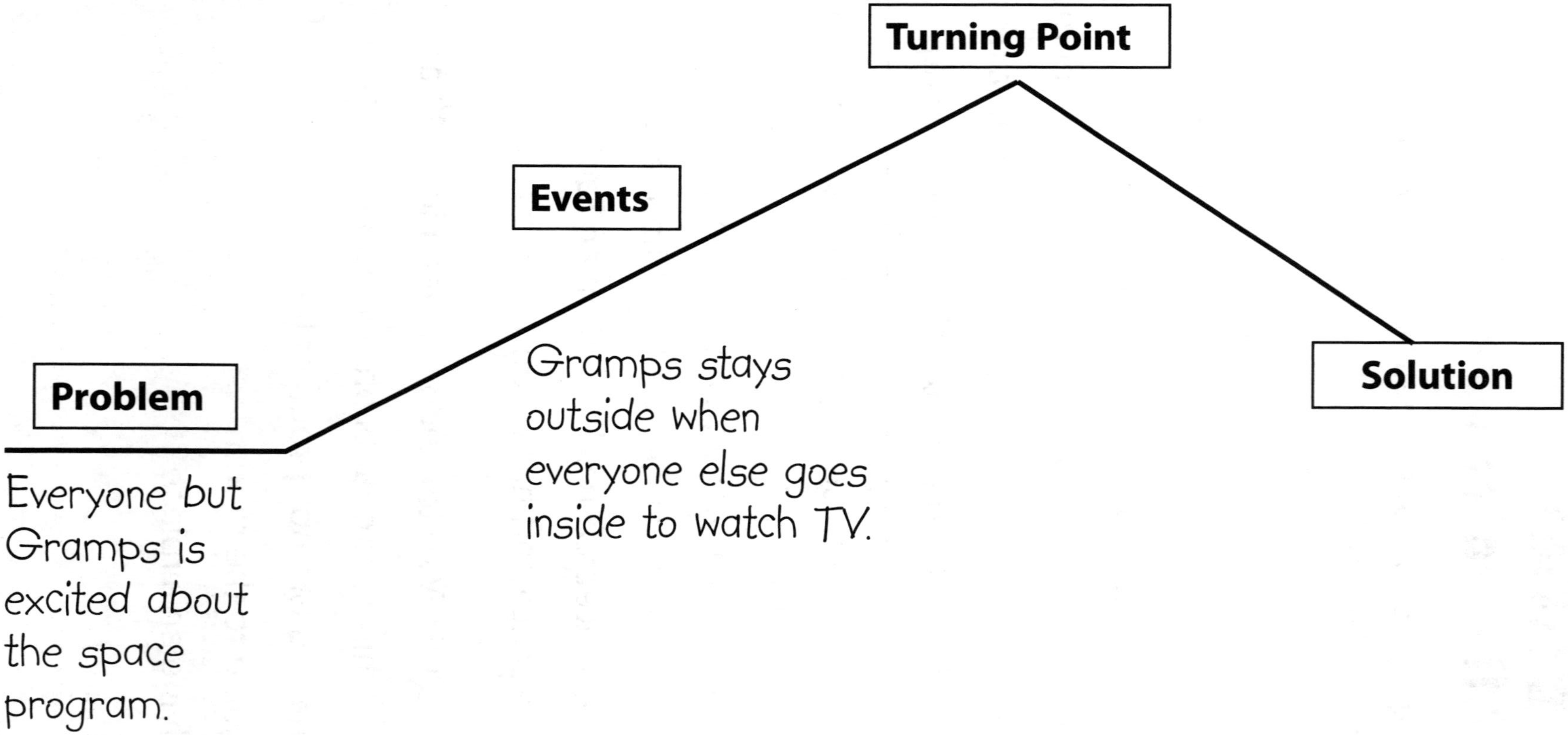

Turning Point

Events

Solution

Problem

Everyone but Gramps is excited about the space program.

Gramps stays outside when everyone else goes inside to watch TV.

Use your plot diagram to retell the story to a partner.

"The Moon Over Star"

Use this passage to practice reading with proper expression.

Later, when it was as quiet as the world ever gets, Gramps   12

and I stood together under the moon.   19

"What's mankind?" I asked him.   24

"It's all of us," he finally said. "It's all of us who've ever lived,   38

all of us still to come."   44

I put my hand in his. "Just think, Gramps, if they could go   57

to the moon, maybe one day I could too!"   66

"Great days," he said, "an astronaut in the family. Who'd a thought?"   78

I smiled in the dark. My gramps was proud of me.   89

From "The Moon Over Star," page 473

Intonation

1 ☐ Does not read with feeling.　　3 ☐ Reads with appropriate feeling for most content.

2 ☐ Reads with some feeling, but does not match content.　　4 ☐ Reads with appropriate feeling for all content.

Accuracy and Rate Formula
Use the formula to measure a reader's accuracy and rate while reading aloud.

_________ − _________ = _________
words attempted　　number of errors　　words correct per minute
in one minute　　　　　　　　　　　(wcpm)

Grammar: Reteach

Cooking Class

Grammar Rules: Adverbs

An **relative adverb** relates a dependent clause to a noun in the main clause.

- *When* relates to a noun of time.
- *Where* relates to a noun of place.
- *Why* relates to a reason for something.

Three o'clock is the time <u>when</u> I take my cooking class.

This is the classroom <u>where</u> I go to the class.

Good food is the reason <u>why</u> I love this class.

Read the sentences below. Circle the relative adverb in each one. Then fill in the correct words to complete the last sentence.

1. This is the table where we read the recipes.
2. The beginning of class is the time when we get our jobs.
3. A broken mixer is the reason why we have to mix the batter by hand.
4. The end of class is the time when we clean up.
5. The sink is the place where I put the dirty bowls.
6. The big mess is the reason why I stayed late.

With a partner, talk about a special class or activity. Take turns using relative adverbs to describe it.

Preposition Clues

Directions:

1. Player 1 tosses a coin onto the set of squares.

2. If the preposition the coin lands on tells a **location**, Player 1 uses the preposition in a sentence describing the location of an object in the classroom. ("This object is *beside* the teacher's desk.")

3. If the preposition describes **when something happens**, Player 1 uses it to describe an event.

4. Teammates guess what the object or event is. Guessers can use other prepositions to ask more questions. ("Is it *on* the floor?" "Is it *before* lunch?")

5. The player who guesses correctly tosses the next coin, and play continues until everyone has had three turns.

above	during	inside
under	from	before
after	behind	outside
next to	between	near
beside	from _____ to _____	over

Grammar: Game

Sort Prepositions

Directions:

1. Write the prepositions from your list in the appropriate column below. You will have two minutes to sort all of your prepositions. Remember: Some prepositions can go in more than one column.

2. Check your chart with a partner. Assign yourself one point for each preposition you sorted correctly.

3. Add all your points and compare your score with some of your classmates' scores.

Location	Time	Direction	Other

Comparison Chart

Compare Fiction and Biography

Compare a story and a biography.

Event or Fact	"The Moon Over Star"	"The First Person on the Moon"
Neil Armstrong was born in 1930.		✓
In 1961, President Kennedy said that America would send people to the moon.	✓	✓
Armstrong, Aldrin, and Collins flew to the moon in the summer of 1969.		
Armstrong was the commander of the mission.		
The first person to walk on the moon was Armstrong.		
The world watched on television.		
Armstrong said, "One small step for man, one giant leap for mankind."		
The astronauts placed a flag on the moon.		
The moon is 240,000 miles from Earth.		

Work with a partner to complete the chart. What other fact or event did you add? Discuss with another team the facts that each selection gave about Armstrong.

The Moon Over Me

Grammar Rules Prepositional Phrases

A prepositional phrase starts with a preposition and ends with a noun or a pronoun. A prepositional phrase can:

show where	in, on, at, over, under, above, below, next to, beside, in front of, behind
show time	after, until, before, during
show direction	into, throughout, up, down, through, across, to
add details	with, to, about, among, except, of, from

Add one or more prepositional phrases to each sentence.

1. I found a book about the moon _____________ .

2. The book was filled _____________ .

3. I was excited to take the book _____________ .

4. We have been studying _____________ .

5. My teacher liked the fact sheet _____________ .

6. My favorite photo is the picture _____________ .

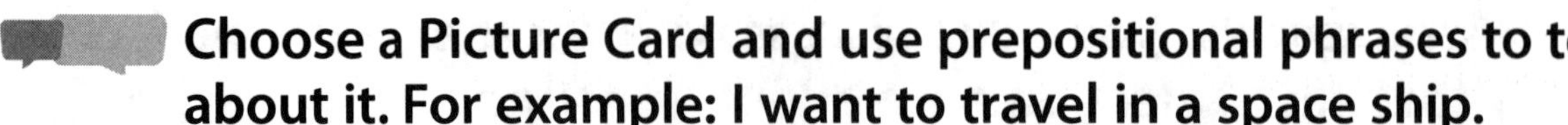 **Choose a Picture Card and use prepositional phrases to tell about it. For example: I want to travel in a space ship.**

The Lunar Landing

by Neil Armstrong, Walter Cronkite, and Edwin Aldrin

*On July 20, 1969, American astronauts Neil Armstrong and Edwin "Buzz" Aldrin became the first humans on the moon. Following is a **transcript** of what Armstrong said as he stepped out of the* Eagle, *the LM or **lunar module**, and down its ladder. At first Armstrong spoke to Aldrin, who was still inside the LM.*

▲ Armstrong and Aldrin left an American flag on the moon.

Armstrong: Okay, I just checked getting back up to that first step, Buzz. It's. . . .The **strut** isn't collapsed too far, but it's adequate to get back up. . . . Takes a pretty good little jump (to get back up to the first step). (Pause) I'm at the foot of the ladder. The LM footpads are only **depressed** in the surface about 1 or 2 inches, although the surface appears to be very, very fine grained as you get close to it. It's almost like a powder. [The] ground mass is very fine. I'm going to step off the LM now. (Long Pause) That's one small step for . . . man; one giant leap for mankind.

Reporter Walter Cronkite described the event live on television.

Cronkite: So there's a foot on the moon, stepping down on the moon. If he's testing that first step, he must be stepping down on the moon at this point. Whoa, look at those pictures—wow! It's a little shadowy, but he said he expected that in the shadow of the lunar module. Armstrong is on the moon—Neil Armstrong, 38-year-old American, standing on the surface of the moon on this July 20th, 1969.

In Other Words

transcript written record

lunar module spaceship that landed on the moon

strut support for the ladder

depressed sank

The Lunar Landing (continued)

Cronkite watched as Buzz Aldrin followed Armstrong down the ladder and became the second man on the moon.

▲ Walter Cronkite watched Armstrong and Aldrin step off the LM onto the surface of the moon.

Cronkite: Aldrin then followed Armstrong out of the LM and into history. There he comes. Watch that last step! I guess he expected that step to **compact** a little bit more and, as a result, it's a long step. And now we have two Americans on the moon. **Three-foot first step** at one-sixth gravity, and look at that!

More than forty-five years later, Buzz Aldrin reflected on the event in his book, Buzz Aldrin: Reaching for the Moon.

Aldrin: Neil and I put on our space suits. Neil climbed out first and descended *Eagle's* ladder to the moon's surface. Everyone listening back on Earth heard Neil's first words: "That's one small step for… man, one giant leap for mankind."

I climbed down the ladder and joined Neil. There was no color on the moon. A flat landscape of rocks and craters stretched in all directions. Everything was gray or white. The shadows and the sky above were as black as the blackest velvet I had ever seen. I exclaimed: **"Magnificent desolation."**

In Other Words

compact push together with the next step

Three-foot first step He easily jumps three feet between the ladder and the ground

Magnificent desolation. Amazing and beautiful emptiness.

Edit and Proofread

Choose the Editing and Proofreading Marks you need to correct the passage. Look for correct usage of:

- prepositions
- prepositional phrases

Editing and Proofreading Marks

∧	Add.
ℐ	Take out.
⌒∧	Move to here.
∧ (comma)	Add comma.
⊙	Add period.

Darkness looms around us. Not a speck of light creeps into the huge

room. We are a planetarium, and the show is starting!

A professor beside the university walks in front of us. "You are

about to travel through the universe," he says outside a deep voice.

"Is everyone ready?" Suddenly images stars appear on a screen

above our heads. We stare in amazement from the starry dome. It is

like looking the night sky, only a thousand times better.

Mysterious music swirls us. It fades, and the professor begins

speaking again. He tells us the images. Then we zoom close to a

star. It's like really being of space! It will be hard to return Earth after

traveling through.

Walking the Dog

Grammar Rules: Prepositions

A **preposition** links a noun or pronoun to other words in a sentence. • Prepositions show location, time, or direction. • Some prepositions have many uses.	I walk the dog <u>on</u> the sidewalk. (location) I can walk the dog <u>until</u> dinner. (time) I walk the dog <u>across</u> the park. (direction) I walk the dog <u>for</u> an hour.
A **prepositional phrase** always begins with a preposition and ends with a noun or pronoun.	I walk the dog <u>to the supermarket.</u>

Read the sentences below. Circle the preposition and underline the prepositional phrase.

1. I walked my dog, Sandy, to the lake.
2. She jumped into the water!
3. I called her and raced around the lake.
4. Finally, she bounced up the steps.
5. She darted behind the bushes.
6. We ran home after the fun.

 **With a partner, talk about the dog's activities during her walk. Use prepositional phrases to describe what she did.**

Saving a Piece of the World

Make a concept map with the answers to the Big Question: What's worth protecting?

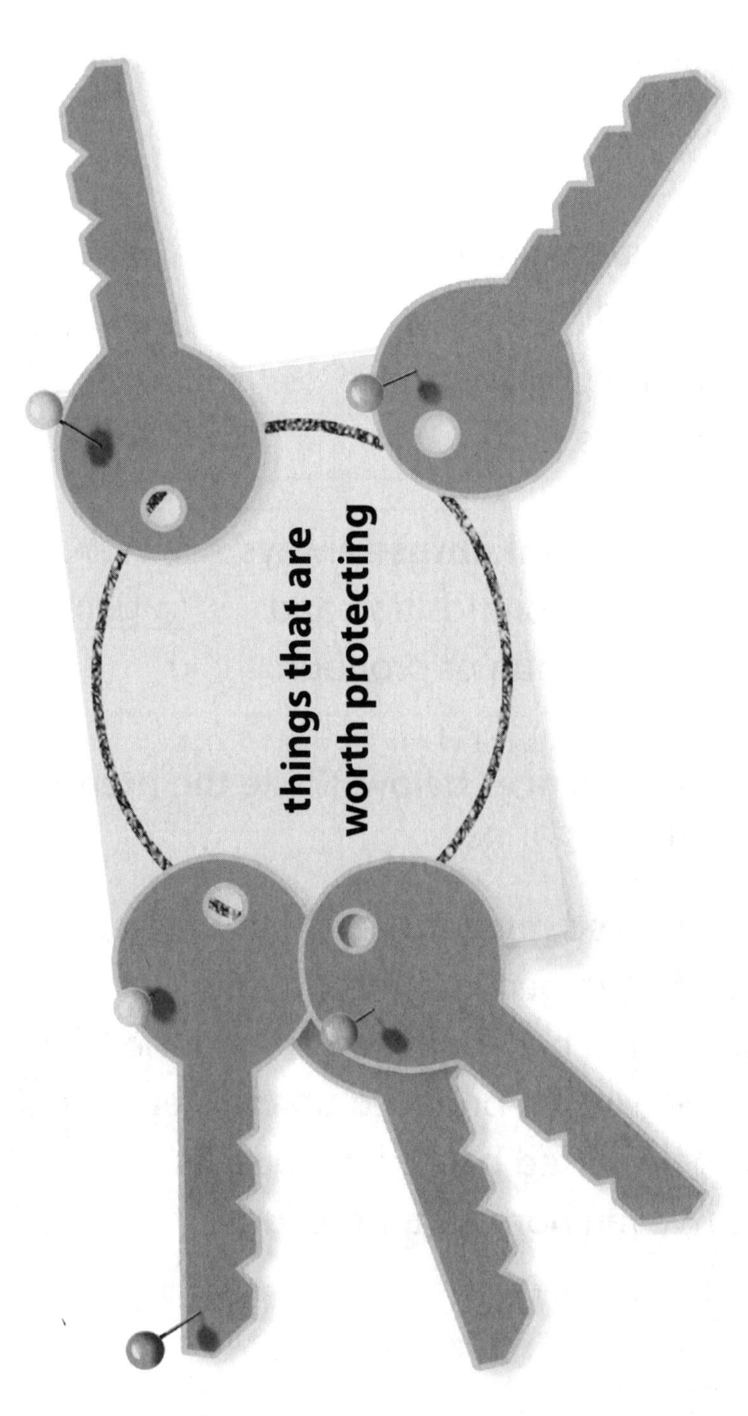

Name _______________________________ Date _______________

Mapping a Goal

Make a goal-and-outcome map about a project that you completed.

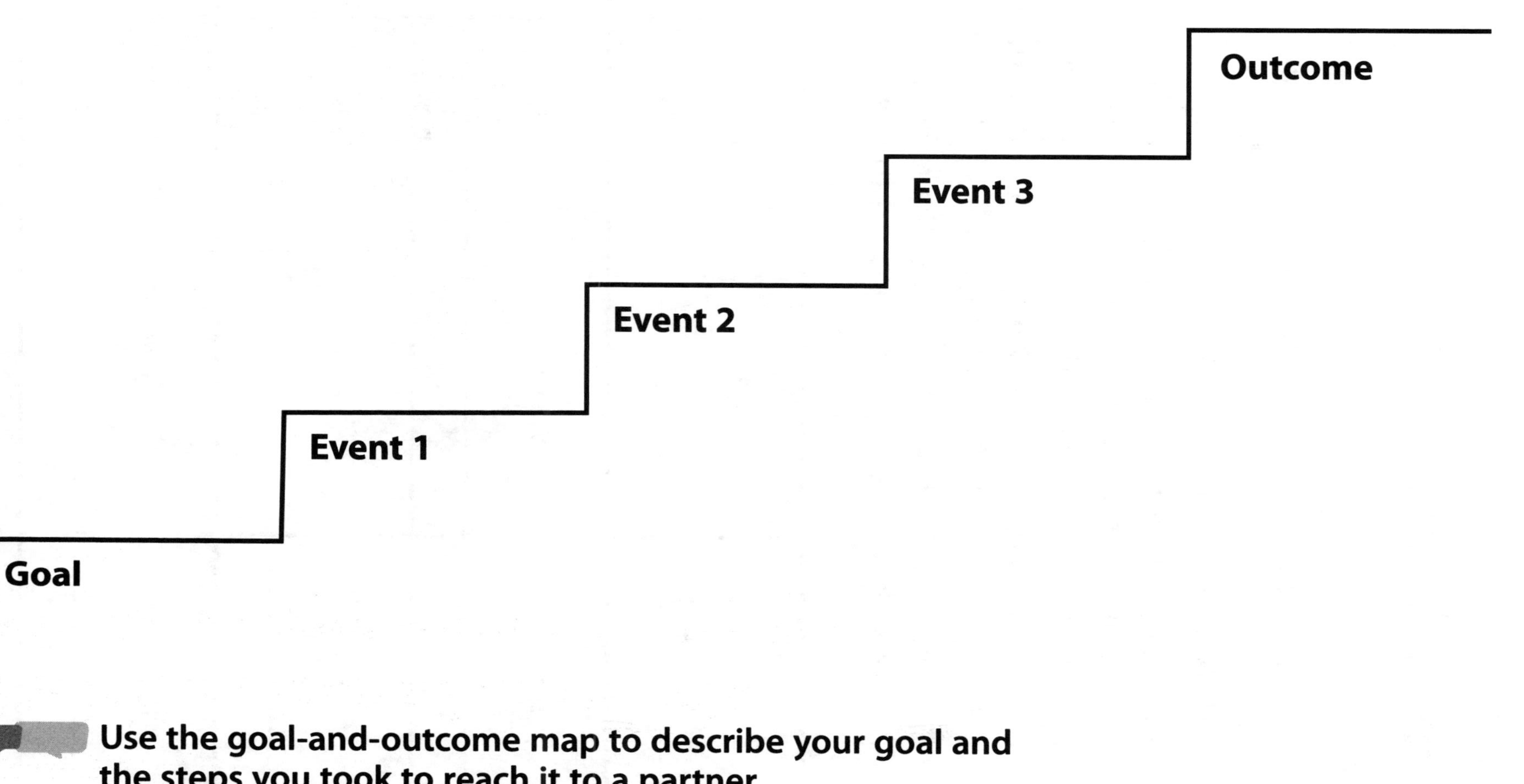

Use the goal-and-outcome map to describe your goal and the steps you took to reach it to a partner.

For use with TE p. T493a

PM8.2

Put It in the Past!

Directions:

1. With your partner, cut 8 index cards in half and write numbers 1 through 16 on separate pieces. Shuffle the cards and stack them face down.

2. Take turns drawing a card. Look for the verb in the grid whose number matches the number on your card. Write the past tense of the verb in the correct square on the grid.

3. Have your partner check the spelling. If it is correct, keep the card. If not, correct the spelling, but set the card aside.

4. The game ends when all the cards have been drawn. The player with more cards at the end of the game wins.

1. call	2. hope	3. live	4. change
5. work	6. use	7. value	8. protect
9. reclaim	10. need	11. remodel	12. inspire
13. plant	14. whistle	15. dream	16. restore

Edit and Proofread

Choose the Editing and Proofreading Marks you need to correct the passage. Look for correct usage of the following:

- regular past tense verbs
- irregular past tense verbs

Editing and Proofreading Marks

∧	Add.
℘	Take out.
⌒∧	Move to here.
∧̣	Add comma.
⊙	Add period.

Last year, the vacant lot next to my apartment building i̶s̶ really a mess. Weeds growed as high as cornstalks. Trash littered the ground. The fence was coverd with graffiti.

One day I decideed to do something about it. I gatherd my friends and suggested that we clean up the place. "We can get rid of the trash, plant flowers, and paint the fence," I say.

Everyone loveed the idea. We hurryed to gather materials— trash bags, garden tools, seeds, paintbrushes and paint. We luged everything to the lot and got going. We worked hard, but all of us enjoyd transforming the lot into a pretty place.

Test-Taking Strategy Practice

Skip and Return to Questions

Read each question about "Buffalo Music." Choose the best answer.

Sample

1 How do you know that Charlie supported Molly's goal even though he told her raising the two calves wouldn't change anything?

Ⓐ Charlie just shook his head at Molly.

Ⓑ Charlie was tired of having wild critters in the dugout.

Ⓒ Charlie didn't waste his breath arguing with Molly.

● Charlie would start the dugout fire every time a new orphan showed up.

2 Where did Billie get the orphaned calves?

Ⓐ The neighbors rescued them.

Ⓑ He found them under a tree.

Ⓒ The hunters gave them to him.

Ⓓ He bought them.

3 What motivates Molly to take care of the buffalo?

Ⓐ She misses the sound of them.

Ⓑ She wants them for meat.

Ⓒ Charlie keeps bringing them home.

Ⓓ She wants them to live in Yellowstone.

Tell a partner how you used the strategy to answer the questions.

Name ___________________________   Date ___________________

"Buffalo Music"

Make a goal-and-outcome map for "Buffalo Music."

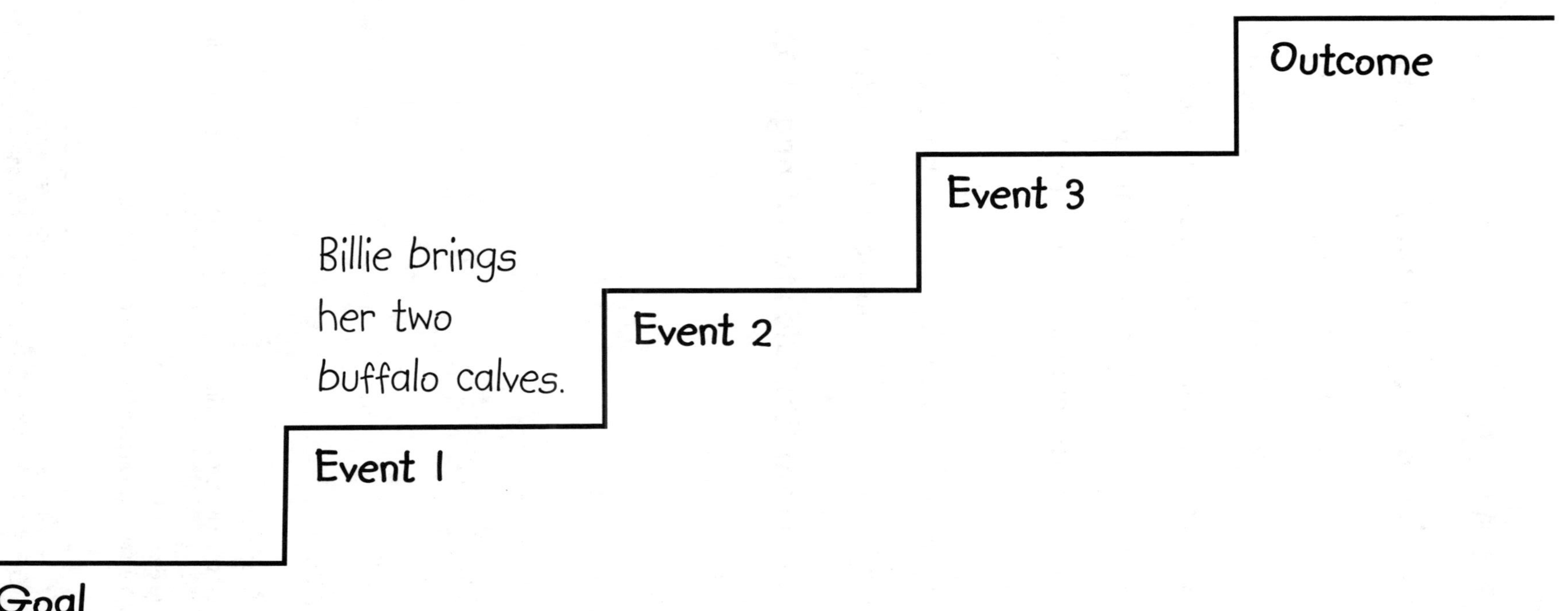

Use the goal-and-outcome map to retell the story to a partner.

Fluency Practice

"Buffalo Music"

Use this passage to practice reading with proper intonation.

That summer, the heat fell as heavy as an angry fist. 11

The trails were deep with dust. The grass cracked like glass 22

underfoot. And everywhere, as far as the eye could see, the 33

bleached bones of the buffalo glistened white in the sun. 43

Within six seasons, the hunters were gone. So was the 53

buffalo music. 55

Oh, those were lonely, silent days! I was sure the only 66

song left in the canyon was the old whistle of the north wind. 79

From "Buffalo Music," page 502

Intonation

| 1 | ☐ Does not change pitch. | 3 | ☐ Changes pitch to match some of the content. |
| 2 | ☐ Changes pitch, but does not match content. | 4 | ☐ Changes pitch to match all of the content. |

Accuracy and Rate Formula

Use the formula to measure a reader's accuracy and rate while reading aloud.

_________ − _________ = _________

words attempted   number of errors   words correct per minute
in one minute   (wcpm)

Trip to the Moon

Grammar Rules: Verbs

The **past tense** form of a regular verb ends with *-ed*. • For verbs that end in silent *e*, drop the e before adding *-ed*. • For verbs that end in one vowel + one consonant, double the final consonant before adding *-ed*. • For verbs that end in a consonant and *y*, change *y* to *i* before adding *-ed*.	The rocket blast<u>ed</u> into the sky. We hop<u>ed</u> to land on the moon We travel<u>led</u> a long way. Valeria cr<u>ied</u> with happiness when we landed.
The **irregular past tense** does not add *-ed*.	I <u>took</u> pictures.

Circle the past-tense verb of the underlined present-tense verb.

The surface of the moon <u>is</u> (was, ised) dusty. Ted <u>try</u> (tryd, tried) to put moon rocks in his bag. We enjoyed the view of Earth. I <u>dig</u> (dug, digged) a hole. Valeria <u>unroll</u> (unroled, unrolled) the flag. Ted <u>place</u> (placied, placed) the flag in the hole. The flag <u>show</u> (showed, showd) that we had been there.

Pick two past-tense verbs from above and write new sentences. Read them to a partner.

From Present to Past

Directions:

1. With your group, write each word below on a separate card. Shuffle the cards and stack them face down.

2. Take turns turning over the top card.

3. Spell the past tense of the verb on your card and use it in a sentence. If your group agrees that you are correct, keep the card. If the group is not sure, check the word in a dictionary. If you were wrong, replace the card in the stack.

4. The game ends when all the cards have been taken. The player with the most cards wins.

make	do	ride	go
say	become	be	begin
buy	come	write	win
take	have	tell	grow

Grammar: Game

What Was Happening?

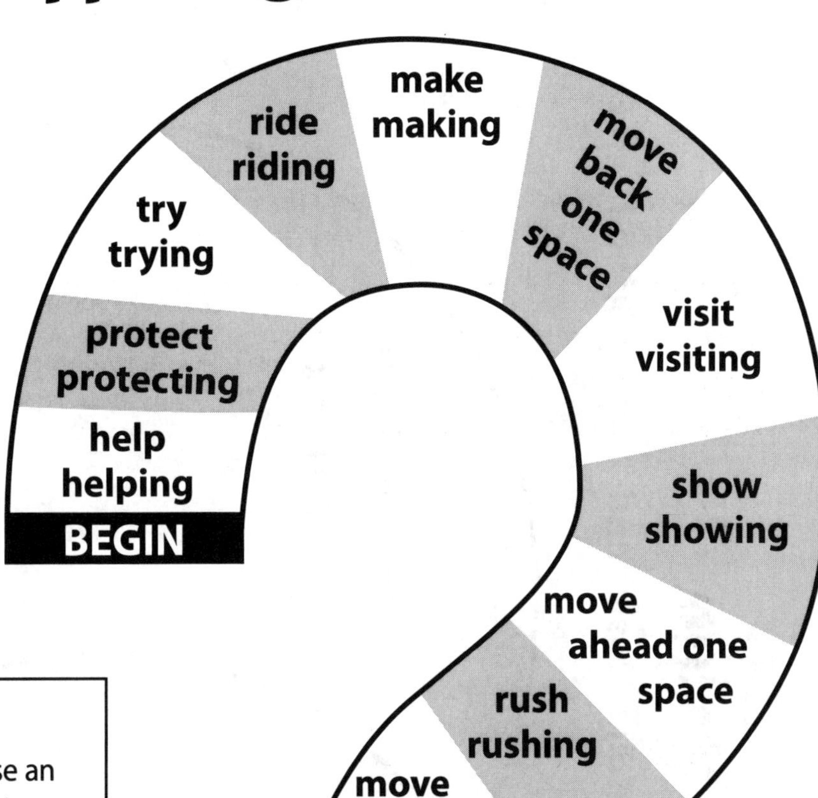

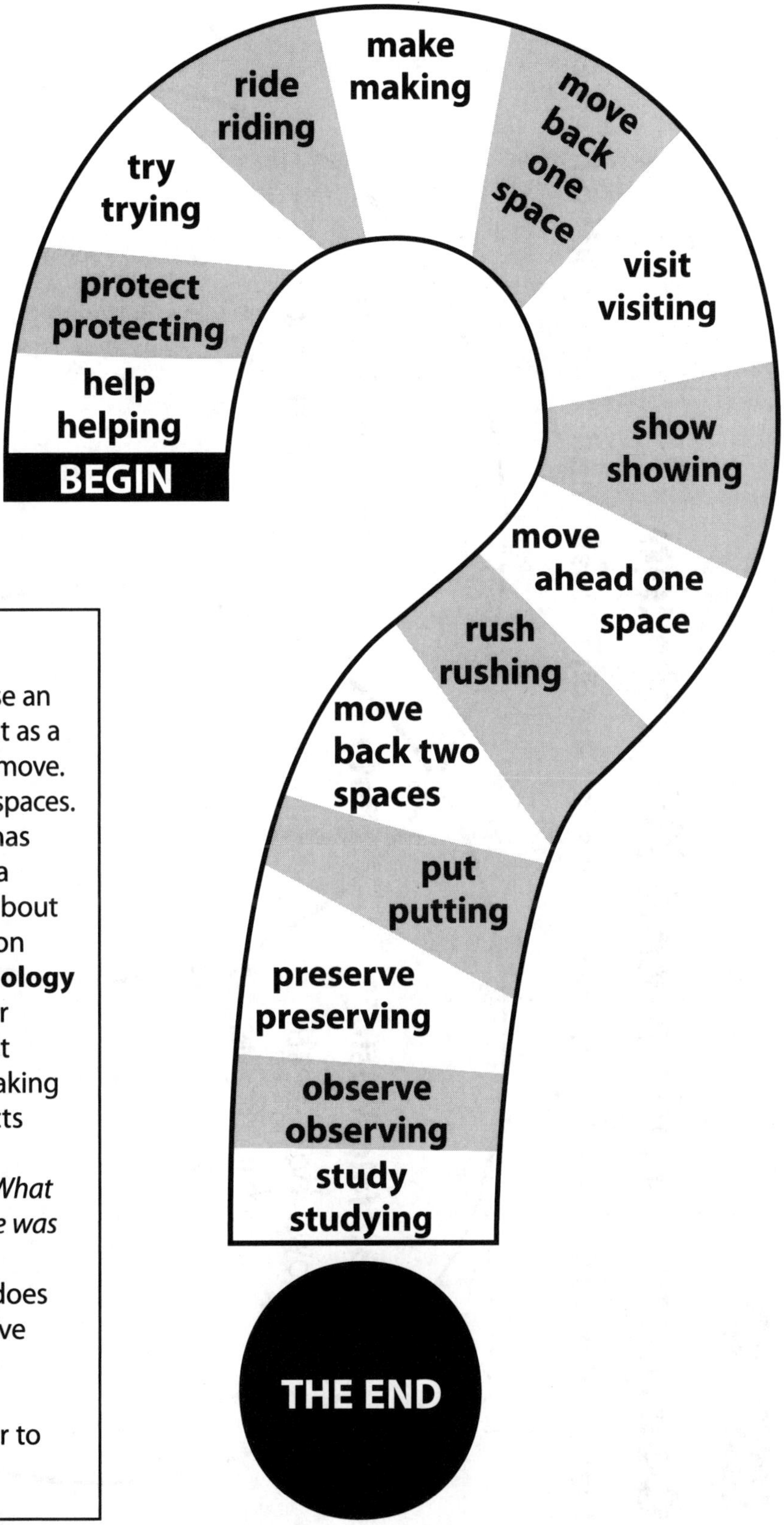

Directions:

1. Play with a small group. Use an eraser or other small object as a game piece. Flip a coin to move. Heads = 1 space, Tails = 2 spaces.
2. If the space you land on has a verb form, use it to ask a question. Ask questions about the photos in "Saving Bison from Extinction" on **Anthology** pages 517–523. The player to your right uses the past progressive to answer, making sure the verbs and subjects agree.
   For example: **Question:** *What was he riding?* **Answer:** *He was riding a horse.*
3. If the space you land on does not have a past-progressive form of a verb, follow the directions on the space.
4. Take turns. The first player to reach THE END wins.

Name ___________________________   Date ___________________________

Compare Fiction and Nonfiction

Make a Venn Diagram to compare ideas in "Buffalo Music" and "Saving Bison from Extinction."

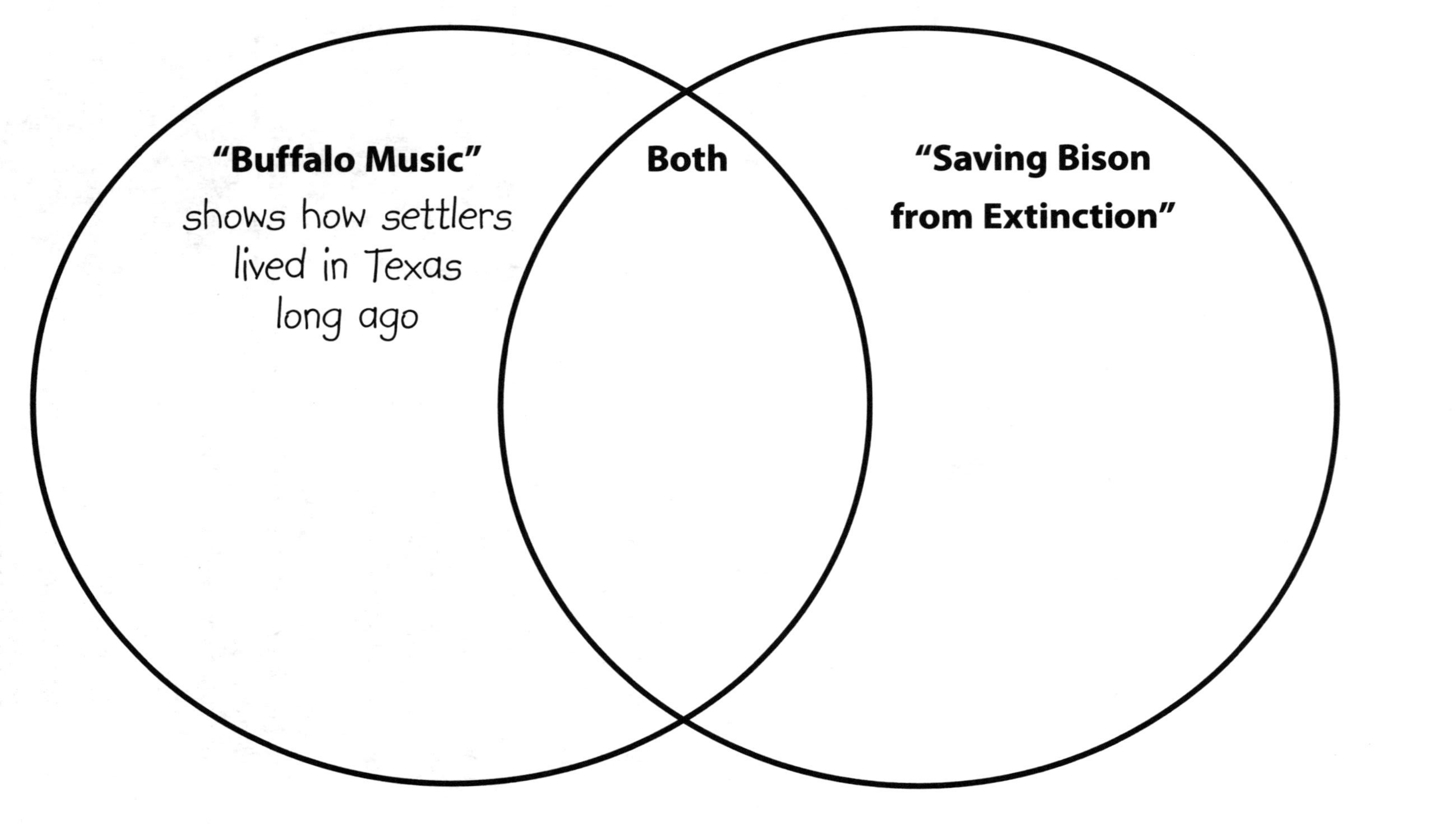

Grammar: Practice

In the Past

Grammar Rules Past Tense

- Add **-ed** to form the past tense of most verbs.
- Drop the final **e** and add **-ed** to verbs like *live* **(lived)**.
- Double the final consonant and add **-ed** to verbs like *hop* **(hopped)**.
- Change the **y** to **i** and add **-ed** to verbs like *cry* **(cried)**.
- Learn the special past–tense forms of irregular verbs like *come* **(came)** and *have* **(had)**.

Write the past tense form of the verb to complete each sentence.

Samuel Walking Coyote was a Native American who ___________ to
(help)

protect the bison. One day, several orphaned calves ___________ into
(walk)

his camp. Walking Coyote ___________ the orphaned calves. Soon,
(raise)

his small herd ___________ . He ___________ his herd to people who
(grow)   (sell)

___________ to let the bison roam free. William Hornaday ___________
(plan)   (try)

to protect the bison, too. Hornaday ___________ a small group of
(bring)

bison to the Bronx Zoo. He ___________ the bison from becoming
(saved)

extinct by forming the American Bison Society.

With your partner, write a paragraph to tell how bison were almost hunted to extinction. Use past tense verbs in your sentences.

Mark-Up Reading

Conservation News

▼ **Protecting Asian Elephants**

Cambodia's Last Elephants?

Vathana Enters the Scene

Low-Cost Plans Bring Success

Protecting Asian Elephants
by Charles Smolar

Cambodia's Last Elephants?

Elephants are an important part of Cambodian culture. But, conflicts between humans and elephants have helped cause Cambodia's elephant population to **plummet**. National Geographic explorer Tuy Sereivathana (known as Vathana) works to protect the few elephants that remain.

Vathana Enters the Scene

Human-elephant conflicts were usually about food. Hungry elephants were attracted to farmer's crops. Farmers killed and injured elephants to protect their crops. Since 2003, Vathana has managed a team to help humans and elephants get along.

Low-Cost Plans Bring Success

Vathana's team taught farmers to raise special crops that they can pick before the elephants even

▲ Vathana works to save Cambodia's elephants.

notice that they are ripe. Noisemakers and fireworks scare the elephants away from farms. These low-cost ideas work! Since 2005, no elephants have died as a result of human-elephant conflicts.

In Other Words

plummet decrease rapidly

The main idea of the article is: _______________________________

____

Mark-Up Reading

Conservation News

▼ **Saving Sonoran Pronghorns**

Race Against Extinction

Preserving Pronghorn Habitat

A Complex Response

Hope for the Future

Saving Sonoran Pronghorns

by Scott Whitman

Race Against Extinction

One of the fastest land animals in North America, Sonoran pronghorns can move like greased lightning, reaching speeds of 60 miles per hour. However, even these speed demons might not be able to outrun the threat of extinction. The population of Sonoran pronghorns' has dropped drastically in recent years and the United States government has listed them as an endangered species. Wildlife biologist Mike Coffeen is on a mission to save Sonoran pronghorns.

Coffeen's help is coming just in time. Today fewer than 100 Sonoran pronghorns live in the wild—just a drop in the bucket compared to the millions that once roamed the West.

▲ The Sonoran pronghorn has been listed as an endangered species since 1967.

Preserving Pronghorn Habitat

New highways and construction projects mean the pronghorns have less space to run and fewer plants to eat. To address this problem, Coffeen and his team have been working tirelessly around the clock to recreate the pronghorns' disappearing habitat on an animal refuge in Arizona.

Mark-Up Reading

Conservation News

▼ Saving Sonoran Pronghorns

Race Against Extinction

Preserving Pronghorn Habitat

A Complex Response

Hope for the Future

Saving Sonoran Pronghorns

A Complex Response

Coffeen's work on this pronghorn refuge shows a complex response to the animals' needs. By bringing in plenty of water and taking care of the plants that the pronghorns eat, Mike and his team keep the pronghorns happy and healthy. However, Coffeen has to be careful not to treat the pronghorns like pets. If he does, they might not be able to survive in the wild again!

Another challenge to the pronghorns is the fences that they must cross when they migrate. Since pronghorns are great runners but not very good jumpers, fences are nearly impossible for them to cross. Coffeen hopes that, over time, all the old fences will be replaced with new fences that pronghorns can pass under.

▲ Fences make migration difficult for Sonoran pronghorns.

Hope for the Future

Although progress is slow, Mike is hopeful that the pronghorn herd will continue to grow. Perhaps we will never see 35 million pronghorns again, but we can definitely protect the ones alive today!

The main idea of the article is: _______________________________________

____

____

Edit and Proofread

Choose the Editing and Proofreading Marks you need to correct the passage. Look for correct usage of the following:

- regular past-tense verbs
- irregular past-tense verbs
- past-progressive verb forms

Editing and Proofreading Marks

∧	Add.
℘	Take out.
⊂⊃∧	Move to here.
∧	Add comma.
⊙	Add period.

"The crows destroied the nest again," Soraya tell Carla with a sigh.

She staring sadly at the shattered nest on the ground.

"The doves don't stand a chance," Carla replyed.

As they talking, the girls pickd up the twigs and leaves scattered on the patio. They gathered the broken eggs, too. "How can we prevent the crows from doing this again?" Soraya askd.

They were think hard when a great idea poped into Carla's mind.

"Let's get one of those wooden owls," she suggesteed.

The next day, they buyed the owl and tieed it in the doves' tree.

From that day on, the crows staied away.

The Class Play

Grammar Rules: Verbs

The **past tense** form of a regular verb ends with -*ed*.	Mrs. Juarez talk<u>ed</u> about the class play.
The **irregular past tense** does not add -*ed*.	She <u>wrote</u> about the play.
A **past-progressive verb** tells about an action that happened over a period of time in the past. Use *was* or *were* and add -*ing*.	I <u>was</u> wonder<u>ing</u> if I should try out.

Circle the correct past tense verb to complete each sentence.

1. Angela (wanted/was wanting) the lead role.
2. Eddie (singed/sang) a song to try out.
3. We (were reading/readed) the script.
4. Mrs. Juarez (listened/listen) to me recite my lines.
5. I (getted/got) the part!

 **With a partner, discuss a class event. Take turns using past-tense verbs to describe it.**

Name ____   Date _______________________

Analyze a Message

Make a fact-and-opinion chart about an ad, poster, or flyer you have seen.

Facts	Opinions

For use with TE p. T527a

PM8.18

Unit 8 | Saving a Piece of the World

Guess Where!

Think of a place where you would like to be. Write clues about the place. Use the present progressive. Have your partner guess the place.

> **Example:** Kids are whizzing down slides. They are playing on swings. Families are eating at picnic tables. Where am I?

____

____

____

____

Answer: You were at ____________________________ .

Now think of a place where you were. Write clues about the place. Use the past progressive. Have your partner guess the place.

> **Example:** Students were studying. My friend was using a computer. I was checking out a book. Where was I?

____

____

____

____

Answer: You were at ____________________________ .

Edit and Proofread

Choose the Editing and Proofreading Marks you need to correct the passage. Look for correct usage of:

- helping verbs
- helping verbs with
  progressive verb forms

Editing and Proofreading Marks

∧	Add.
℘	Take out.
⌒∧	Move to here.
/	Make lowercase.
≡	Capitalize.

Right now I *am* walking down Ramos Street. It is the oldest street in our town. A few years ago, some people talking about putting a parking lot there. Other people said no. "We save must Ramos Street!" they cried. "We save an important part of our heritage if we could rescue Ramos Street."

It take did a lot of money to buy the old buildings and save the street. Local citizens collecting money for months. "Will we reach our goal!" they declared, and they finally did.

Today Ramos Street is help the community. Tourists come can to Ramos Street and have a wonderful time. Should you come, too!

Revise and Edit

Revise and edit the summaries of "The Key Holders of Kabul."

Sample

> **1** (1) I read an article called "The Key Holders of Kabul." (2) It were about the key holders of the National Museum in Kabul, Afghanistan. (3) It is there responsibility to protect valuable objects. (4) The objects was more valuable than gold.
>
> (1) I read an article called "The Key Holders of Kabul." (2) It was about the key holders of the National Museum in Kabul, Afghanistan. (3) It is their responsibility to protect valuable objects. (4) The objects were more valuable than gold.

2 (1) Fredrik Hiebert work with a Russian archaeologist. (2) He learn about priceless artifacts from Afghanistan. (3) Fredrik want to see them but they lost during a war. (4) He founded out 20 years later they were hidden. (5) Fredrik is invited to watch the opening of the boxes. (6) Everyone happy? (7) When they saw the treasures.

____

____

____

____

____

Tell a partner how you used the strategy to revise.

PM8.21

Name ____ Date _________________________

"The Key Holders of Kabul"

Complete a fact-and-opinion chart about "The Key Holders of Kabul."

Facts	Opinions
In 1987, I went to Central Asia.	After hearing Sarianidi's story, I knew the objects he had found were remarkable.

 **Use your fact-and-opinion chart to analyze the personal narrative for your partner.**

     Unit 8 | Saving a Piece of the World

"The Key Holders of Kabul"

Use this passage to practice reading with appropriate phrasing.

In 1979, the Soviet Union invaded Afghanistan. Sarianidi wanted   9

to protect the treasures he had uncovered. Secretly, he moved them   20

to the National Museum in Kabul.   26

The fight against the Soviets became a civil war. Within two years,   38

a museum in another Afghan city was robbed. Workers at the National   50

Museum did not want their treasures to be lost, too.   60

In 1988, the museum key holders in Kabul packed and labeled   71

their most valuable objects. They hid them in a vault in the presidential   84

palace in Kabul. The key holders kept their secret well. The Afghan   96

people and the rest of the world believed the artifacts had disappeared.   108

From "The Key Holders of Kabul," page 541

Intonation

1 ☐ Rarely pauses while reading the text.   3 ☐ Frequently pauses at appropriate points in the text.

2 ☐ Occasionally pauses while reading the text.   4 ☐ Consistently pauses at all appropriate points in the text.

Accuracy and Rate Formula
Use the formula to measure a reader's accuracy and rate while reading aloud.

_______________	−	_______________	=	_______________
words attempted in one minute		number of errors		words correct per minute (wcpm)

My Trip to Visit Grandma

Grammar Rules: Verbs

Helping verbs help verbs show • ability (*can*) • possibility (*could, may, might*) • opinion (*must, should*) • permission (*may, must*) • present, future, or past (*will/would, do/does/did,* *have/has/had*).	I <u>can</u> take a plane. I <u>may</u> sit by the window. I <u>should</u> have a good time! I <u>will</u> go to the beach. We <u>have</u> enjoyed the ocean.
Present-progressive uses helping verbs *am, is,* or *are.* **Past-progressive** uses the helping verbs *was* or *were.*	The plane <u>is</u> fly<u>ing</u> high. I <u>was</u> read<u>ing</u> a book.

Underline the helping verb. Circle the verb it helps.

1. Grandma must meet me at the airport.
2. I was waving to her.
3. She will take me to her house.
4. We may walk on the beach.
5. I do enjoy visiting Grandma!

With a partner, talk about a past trip. Take turns using helping verbs to describe it.

Imagine This!

1. Play in groups of 3 to 5. One student is the referee. The others are players.

2. Each group has nine Language Builder Picture Cards that show people working to preserve cultural or natural treasures.

3. Taking turns, each player draws a card from the deck. The player then uses future progressive verbs to tell what one or more of the people in the picture will be doing in the future.

4. If the player uses the future progressive correctly, he or she keeps the card. If not, the card goes back on the deck. The referee decides.

5. Play until all of the cards have been used. Then, if time allows, play again!

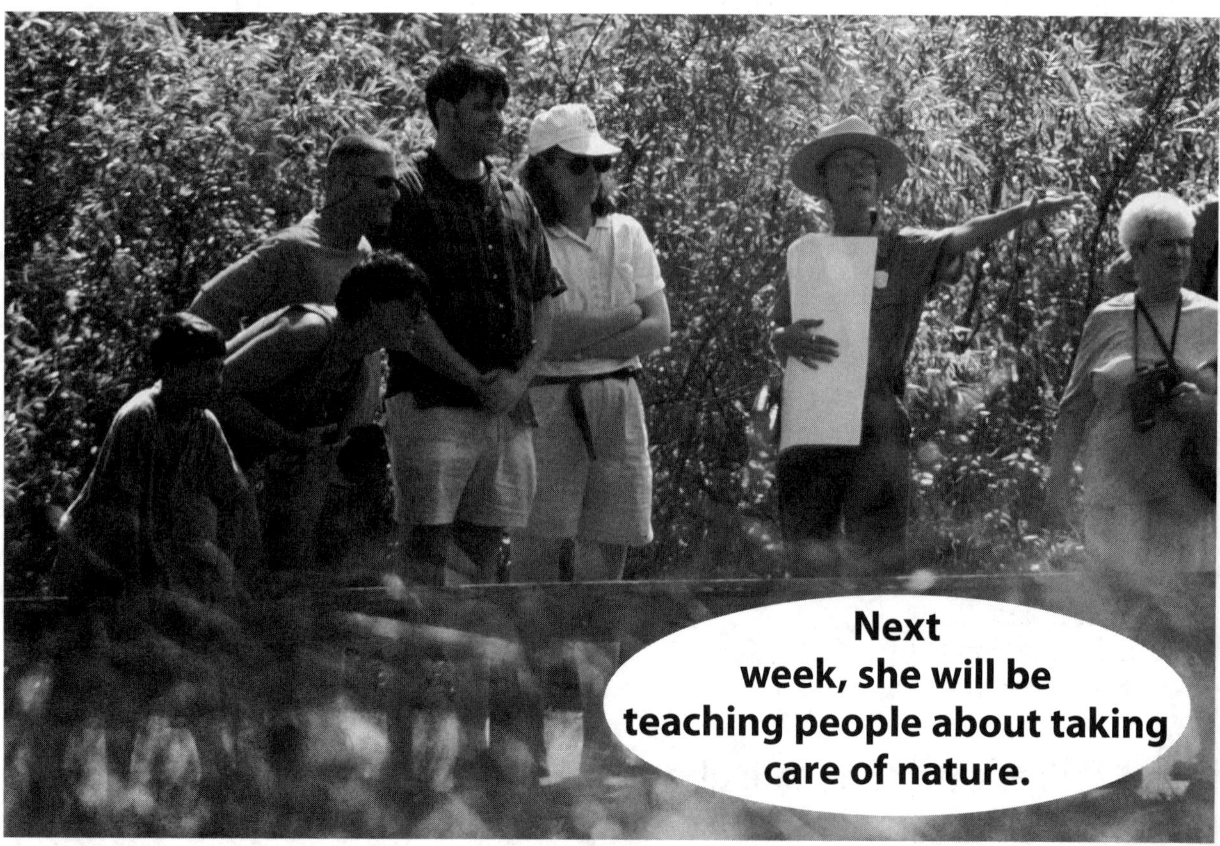

Think of the Future!

Directions:

1. Take turns with your partner spinning the paper clip.

2. Read aloud the sentence the paper clip points to. Then repeat the sentence, but change it to the future tense.

3. Use *am going to, is going to, are going to,* or *will* before the main verb. Drop final *-s* from the main verb, if necessary.

4. Play until you have changed all the sentences.

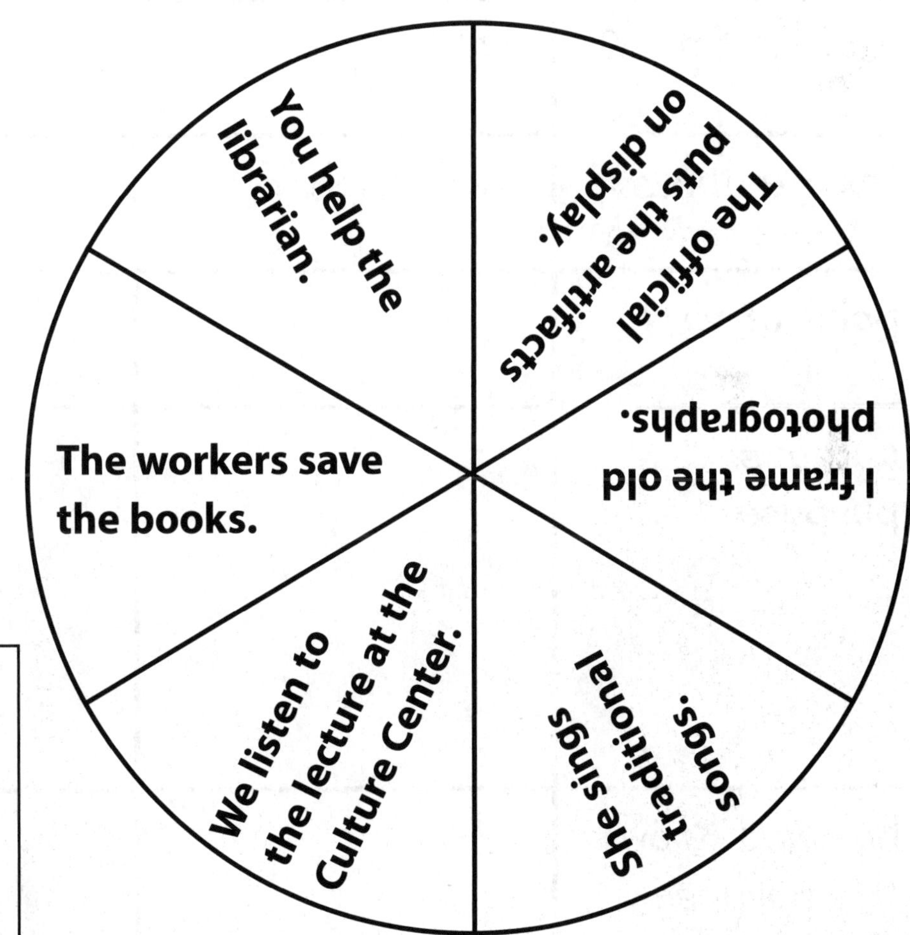

Make a Spinner

1. Put a paper clip over the center of the spinner.

2. Touch the point of a pencil on the middle of the wheel and through the loop of the paper clip.

3. Spin the paper clip to make a spinner.

Compare Features

Make a comparison chart to compare features of an informational text and a literary text.

	"The Key Holders of Kabul"	"The Librarian of Basra"
genre	personal narrative	
real or fiction?	real	
text features	photographs	
point of view		
author's purpose		
how you know the purpose		

A Library in Your Future

Grammar Rules Future Tense

1. Use the helping verb **will** along with a main verb.

   Our library **will move** to a bigger building.

2. Use **am going to**, **is going to**, or **are going to** with a main verb.

   I **am going to like** the new building.

   It **is going to have** room for more books.

   Officials **are going to offer** more programs.

Complete each sentence with the future tense. Use the main verb in parentheses.

1. The library ___*will extend*___ its hours.
   (extend)

2. It _______________ early on Saturdays.
   (open)

3. Two teachers _______________ there after school.
   (work)

4. They _______________ students with their homework.
   (help)

5. The librarian _______________ a movie section.
   (offer)

6. You _______________ movies just like you do books!
   (borrow)

Talk with a partner about the larger library. What else will people be able to do there?

Mark-Up Reading

The Two Brothers
retold by Arman Khan

Once there were two brothers, Ahmed and Ali. Ahmed became a servant of the **sultan**. He lived in the palace and wore a silken robe tied with a glittering belt. He obeyed the orders of those at court day and night. Ali was a laborer who lived in a simple home. Ahmed visited Ali to show his poor brother how well he had done by becoming a servant.

Dressed beautifully, Ahmed strode grandly to where Ali sat in a patched robe. "Why don't you do what I've done?" said Ahmed. "You will live in the palace and wear fine clothes."

"I'd rather wear a patched robe," Ali replied, "than dress in

gleaming silk and run silly erra for sneering people! I value my self-respect."

Ahmed returned to the pala but his life there never felt as grand again.

To this day, Iranian people say, "It is better to be free with just a crust of bread than to bow as a servant to get more."

In Other Words

sultan a ruler in an Arabic country

Proverb Chart

What Ahmed thinks at first	What Ahmed thinks at the end	What the proverb means

Mark-Up Reading

The Short Prince
retold by Arman Khan

There was once a prince named Hassan who was very short and very plain. By contrast, his brothers were tall and handsome. One day all of these princes stood in a row in front of their father the king. As the king's eyes moved along the line of his sons, he smiled at what he saw until he reached Prince Hassan. Hassan knew he didn't look much like a prince and sadly watched his father's smile vanish.

Suddenly an idea occurred to Prince Hassan. He first reminded his father of an old but respected law: "Although the elephant is much larger than the sheep, we eat lamb, but not elephant."

When he saw his father's frown replaced by a smile at his son's

wisdom, Prince Hassan added, "I'd rather be known for my wits than my size. Better to be small and clever than tall and stupid."

To this day, Afghani people still say, "Not everything that is higher in stature is higher in value."

Proverb Chart

What Hassan's father thinks at first	What Hassan's father thinks at the end	What the proverb means

The Terrified Servant

retold by Arman Khan

A king's servant once sailed on a small boat with his master. The servant had never been at sea before and was frightened by the motion of the boat. He became so terrified that he started to moan and tremble. When no one else could calm him, a wise man offered to solve the problem by throwing the servant overboard. The king agreed.

The servant sank below the waves several times and surfaced, sputtering and gasping. Finally, those on the boat grabbed him by the hair and dragged him aboard. At once, the servant sat down and remained calm for the rest of the voyage.

The king later asked his serva[nt] why the motion of the boat no longer frightened him. He said, "Once I met the bigger fear of drowning, my lord, I conquered my smaller fear of the boat."

In Iran today, people still say, "The drowning man is not troubled by rain."

Proverb Chart

What the servant thinks at first	What the servant thinks at the end	What the proverb means

Edit and Proofread

Choose the Editing and Proofreading Marks you need to correct the passage. Look for correct usage of the following:

- the future progressive
- the future tense

Editing and Proofreading Marks

∧	Add.
ℐ	Take out.
⟳∧	Move to here.
⋏	Add comma.
⊙	Add period.

"This summer we will be visit Mesa Verde National Park," Dad said to my sister, Ann, and me. "We are go to see many archaeological sites. You is going to love the cliff dwellings!"

"When we go?" my sister and I asked eagerly.

"We take our vacation the last week in July," Mom said.

"The cliff dwellings are really old!" I exclaimed. "I are going to bring my camera!"

"We also will seeing how the people lived then," Dad added. "We learn will a lot about an ancient culture that existed close to where we live."

I'm Moving!

Grammar Rules: Future

The **future tense** of a verb tells about an event that will happen in the future. • Use *will* before the main verb. • Or use *am/is/are + going to* before the main verb.	I <u>will</u> move tomorrow. We <u>are going to</u> move tomorrow.
The **future progressive** tells about an action that will happen over time in the future. Use *will + be + -ing* for the main verb.	I <u>will be</u> attend<u>ing</u> a new school.

Circle the future tense verb in each sentence.

1. I will pack all of my clothes tonight.
2. Mom will drive to the new house tomorrow.
3. We are going to need a moving truck.
4. I am going to decorate my room next week.
5. I will be meeting new friends soon.

 **With a partner, talk about what you are doing next weekend. Take turns using future-tense verbs to tell about your plans.**